Swami
Abhishiktananda

ॐ

# MODERN SPIRITUAL MASTERS
Robert Ellsberg, Series Editor

*Already published:*

Dietrich Bonhoeffer (edited by Robert Coles)
Simone Weil (edited by Eric O. Springsted)
Henri Nouwen (edited by Robert A. Jonas)
Pierre Teilhard de Chardin (edited by Ursula King)
Anthony de Mello (edited by William Dych, S.J.)
Charles de Foucauld (edited by Robert Ellsberg)
Oscar Romero (by Marie Dennis, Rennie Golden, and Scott Wright)
Eberhard Arnold (edited by Johann Christoph Arnold)
Thomas Merton (edited by Christine M. Bochen)
Thich Nhat Hanh (edited by Robert Ellsberg)
Rufus Jones (edited by Kerry Walters)
Mother Teresa (edited by Jean Maalouf)
Edith Stein (edited by John Sullivan, O.C.D.)
John Main (edited by Laurence Freeman)
Mohandas Gandhi (edited by John Dear)
Mother Maria Skobtsova (introduction by Jim Forest)
Evelyn Underhill (edited by Emilie Griffin)
St. Thérèse of Lisieux (edited by Mary Frohlich)
Flannery O'Connor (edited by Robert Ellsberg)
Clarence Jordan (edited by Joyce Hollyday)
G. K. Chesterton (edited by William Griffin)
Alfred Delp, S.J. (introduction by Thomas Merton)
Bede Griffiths (edited by Thomas Matus)
Karl Rahner (edited by Philip Endean)
Sadhu Sundar Singh (edited by Charles E. Moore)
Pedro Arrupe (edited by Kevin F. Burke, S.J.)
Romano Guardini (edited by Robert A. Krieg)
Albert Schweitzer (edited by James Brabazon)
Caryll Houselander (edited by Wendy M. Wright)
Brother Roger of Taizé (edited by Marcello Fidanzio)
Dorothee Soelle (edited by Dianne L. Oliver)
Leo Tolstoy (edited by Charles E. Moore)
Howard Thurman (edited by Luther E. Smith, Jr.)

MODERN SPIRITUAL MASTERS SERIES

# Swami Abhishiktananda

Essential Writings

ॐ

Selected with an Introduction by
SHIRLEY DU BOULAY

ORBIS BOOKS
Maryknoll, New York 10545

Founded in 1970, Orbis Books endeavors to publish works that enlighten the mind, nourish the spirit, and challenge the conscience. The publishing arm of the Maryknoll Fathers and Brothers, Orbis seeks to explore the global dimensions of the Christian faith and mission, to invite dialogue with diverse cultures and religious traditions, and to serve the cause of reconciliation and peace. The books published reflect the views of their authors and do not represent the official position of the Maryknoll Society. To learn more about Maryknoll and Orbis Books, please visit our website at www.maryknoll.org.

Copyright © 2006 by Shirley du Boulay.

Selections from the writings of Swami Abhishiktananda are used with permission and by arrangement with the Abhishiktananda Society.

Grateful acknowledgment is made to ISPCK (New Delhi, India) for permission to reprint excerpts from *The Secret of Arunachala* and *Hindu-Christian Meeting Point*, and to Les editions du Cerf, for excerpts from Henri Le Saux, *Lettres d'un Sannyasi Chrétien à Joseph Lemarié*.

An effort has been made to clear all permissions for this volume. The publisher regrets any omissions, which will be corrected in a future printing.

Published by Orbis Books, Maryknoll, NY 10545-0308.

All rights reserved.

No part of this publication may be reproduced or transmitted in any form or by any means, electronic or mechanical, including photocopying, recording, or any information storage or retrieval system, without prior permission in writing from the publisher.

Queries regarding rights and permissions should be addressed to:
Orbis Books, P.O. Box 308, Maryknoll, NY 10545-0308.

Manufactured in the United States of America.

**Library of Congress Cataloging-in-Publication Data**
Abhishiktananda, Swami, 1910-1973.
 [Selections. English. 2007]
 Swami Abhishiktananda : essential writings / selected with an introduction by Shirley du Boulay.
   p. cm. – (Modern spiritual masters series)
 ISBN-13: 978-1-57075-695-5 (pbk.)
 1. Christianity and other religions – Hinduism. 2. Hinduism – Relations – Christianity. 3. Spirituality. 4. Spiritual life – Christianity. 5. Spiritual life – Hinduism. I. Du Boulay, Shirley. II. Title. III. Title: Essential writings.
BR128.B8A2413 2007
261.2'45 – dc22
                                                                            2006030802

# Contents

| | |
|---|---|
| Sources | 9 |
| Abbreviations | 11 |
| Glossary | 13 |
| Introduction | 19 |
| | |
| 1. BENEDICTINE MONK | 43 |
|    *Brittany* | 43 |
|    *Vocation* | 44 |
|    *Letter to Louisette* | 45 |
|    *Father Jules Monchanin* | 48 |
|    *Fulfillment Theology* | 52 |
| | |
| 2. ADVAITA | 56 |
|    *Ramana Maharshi: "The Unique Sage of the Eternal India"* | 56 |
|    *Ramana Maharshi's Way* | 59 |
|    *Ramana Maharshi — The Quest of the Self* | 61 |
|    *Advaita — A Definition* | 61 |
|    *The Challenge Christianity and* Advaita *Present to Each Other* | 63 |
|    *Christian and Vedantic Ascesis* | 65 |
|    *Simply Becoming Aware* | 66 |
|    *Man Is Truly Himself* | 69 |
|    *There Is Only Being* | 70 |
|    *Eternity* | 71 |
|    *Eternity in the Present Moment* | 72 |
|    *Goal of the Universe* | 72 |
|    *Being* | 73 |

## 3. EAST-WEST

| | |
|---|---|
| Advaita *and the Religions* | 75 |
| *The Advaitic Dilemma* | 77 |
| *Why Name the Mystery?* | 78 |
| *The West's Interest in the East* | 78 |
| *The Challenge Presented to Christianity* | 81 |
| *A Call to the Church* | 82 |
| *The Tension between Christianity and Hindu* Advaita | 83 |
| *Responses to* Saccidananda | 85 |
| *Tensions* | 86 |

## 4. IMMERSION IN HINDUISM

| | |
|---|---|
| *Pray to Be Simply Transparent* | 88 |
| *The Grace of India* | 92 |
| *Morning Worship* | 97 |
| *Evening Worship* | 98 |
| *Night Prayers* | 101 |
| *Christ the* Sad-Guru *(True Master)* | 101 |
| *Meeting the Guru* | 104 |
| *Greeting the Guru* | 108 |
| *The Effect of Meeting Sri Gnanananda* | 109 |
| *Christ as Guru* | 110 |
| *The Mystery of the Guru* | 111 |
| *The Guru in the Depth of the Heart* | 113 |
| *The Secret of the Guru* | 114 |
| *Pilgrimage* — A Definition | 115 |
| *Setting Off* | 116 |
| *Ascent to Gangotri* | 117 |
| Sadhus | 118 |
| *The Cosmic Covenant* | 119 |
| *Review of* Hindu-Christian Meeting Point | 121 |
| *Hindu-Christian Dialogue Postponed* | 125 |

## 5. THE LIFE OF THE HERMIT — 129
*The Ideal of the* Sannyasi — 129
*Sannyasa* — 130
*Surrender* — 131
*"Naked as a Stone Is Naked"* — 133
*Silence* — 136
*Solitude* — 139
*The Role of Contemplatives* — 141
*Solitude and Emptying* — 142
*The Great Solitude within the Soul* — 143
*From "Esseulement"* — 144
*The Call of the Within* — 148

## 6. CHRISTIANITY — 150
*What Is a Christian?* — 150
*Is It Possible to Live according to the Gospel?* — 155
*"My Father and I Are One"* — 157
*Jesus* — 158
*Jesus, the True Guru* — 159
*Jesus in* Advaita — 159
*For Ascension Day* — 160
*Christ and the Church* — 161
*Saccidananda — A Definition* — 161
*The Trinity* — 164
*The Two Experiences of the Trinity and of Saccidananda* — 164
*Mass* — 166

## 7. GOD — 169
*The Existence of God* — 169
*The Essential Void* — 170
*The Secret of the Within* — 171

|   |   |   |
|---|---|---|
| | *The Meeting of Man with God* | 172 |
| | *Contemplation of the Transcendent-Immanent God* | 172 |
| | *Everywhere He Is, and Only He* | 174 |
| | *Seek God* | 178 |
| 8. | PRAYER | 180 |
| | *God's Presence* | 180 |
| | *Prayer — an Act of Faith* | 182 |
| | *Prayer — God Is beyond Form* | 183 |
| | *God in Creation* | 184 |
| | *The Prayer of the Name* | 184 |
| | *The Primacy of Contemplation* | 187 |
| | *Advaitic Prayer* | 188 |
| | *OM* | 189 |
| | *The Prayer of Silence* | 190 |
| 9. | AWAKENING | 193 |
| | Satori | 193 |
| | *Dazzled* | 194 |
| | *Only for the Strong* | 194 |
| | *The Present Moment* | 195 |
| | *Beyond All Signs* | 196 |
| | *Extracts from Abhishiktananda's* Spiritual Diary | 199 |
| | *The Only Real Self* | 203 |
| | *I Am* | 204 |
| | *Beyond Words* | 205 |

# Sources

*Abbreviations*

| | |
|---|---|
| *Diary* | *Ascent to the Depth of the Heart: The Spiritual Diary of Swami Abhishiktananda.* Edited by Raimon Panikkar. Translated by David Fleming and James Stuart. Delhi: ISPCK, 1998. |
| *Further Shore* | *The Further Shore: Three Essays.* Reprinted with extra material. Delhi: ISPCK, 1970. |
| *Guru* | *Guru and Disciple: An Encounter with Sri Gnanananda, a Contemporary Spiritual Master.* First English edition, London: SPCK, 1974. |
| *Lettres* | *Lettres d'un sannyasi chrétien à Joseph Lemarié.* Paris: Editions du Cerf, 1999. |
| *Life* | *Swami Abhishiktananda: His Life Told through His Letters.* Edited by James Stuart. Delhi: ISPCK, 1989. |
| *LS&T* | *Letters Spiritual and Theological 1953–1973.* Kergonan Archives. |
| *Meeting Point* | *Hindu-Christian Meeting Point: Within the Cave of the Heart.* Delhi: ISPCK, 1983. |
| *Mountain* | *The Mountain of the Lord: Pilgrimage to Gangotri.* New edition. Delhi: ISPCK, 1990. |
| *Prayer* | *Prayer.* New edition. Delhi: ISPCK, 1999. |

| | |
|---|---|
| *Saccidananda* | *Saccidananda: A Christian Approach to Advaitic Experience.* Delhi: ISPCK, 1997. First English edition, 1974. Revised Edition 1984. |
| *Secret* | *The Secret of Arunachala: A Christian Hermit on Shiva's Holy Mountain.* Revised edition. Delhi: ISPCK, 1979. |

## Collections

| | |
|---|---|
| A. le B. Coll. | Agnès le Bris Collection |
| ALA | Abhishiktananda Library and Archives |
| KA | Kergonan Archives |
| MR Coll. | Murray Rogers Collection |

## Miscellaneous Articles

"Esseulement," a chapter in *Intériorité et révélation: Essais théologiques.* Sisteron: Editions Présence, 1982.

"Initiations à la spiritualité des Upanishads," *Guhantara.* Sisteron: Editions Présence, 1979.

A Letter from India, written with C. Murray Rogers, *One in Christ.* vol. 3, 1967.

*Practical Anthropology* 18, no. 6 (November–December 1971).

# Abbreviations

| | |
|---|---|
| AMS | Ann-Marie Stokes |
| AG | Mme A.-L. Guguen-Le Saux |
| BB | Bettina Bäumer |
| FT | Mother Françoise-Thérèse, Prioress of Lisieux |
| JL | Canon Joseph Lemarié |
| JM | Father Jules Monchanin |
| MC | Marc Chaduc |
| MT | Sr. Marie-Thérèse Le Saux |
| OB | Odette Bauman-Despeigne |
| RM | Father R. Macé |
| RP | Dr. Raimon Panikkar |
| SETU | Bulletin of the Abhishiktananda Society |
| TJ | A Carmelite of Lisieux, later in India |
| TL | Sr. Thérèse de Jésus (Lemoine) |

# Glossary

Editor's Note: Swami Abhishiktananda often made references in Sanskrit; he was often, indeed, thinking in Sanskrit. For ease of reading I have removed those words where the meaning is already clear in the English. Where it has seemed better to leave the Sanskrit word I have put the translation in the glossary.

*acharya:* master, teacher, head of an ashram

*acosmic:* literally, denial of a universe apart from God

*advaita:* non-duality

*aham:* I, myself

*aham Brahma asmi:* "I am Brahman"; one of the "great sentences" of the Upanishads, known as *mahāvākya*

*ahamkara:* the sense of oneself as an individual

*akhanda:* indivisible

*anjali:* greeting with the palms of the hands together

*asparsa:* without contact, without attachment

*atman:* the Self, the ultimate ground at once in the human being and in the universe

*atmavid:* one who knows the Self, a sage, *Bhagavan,* Lord

*bhakti:* loving devotion

**Brahma, Vishnu, and Shiva:** respectively the Creator, the Conserver and Protector of the world, the Destroyer; the three forms taken by the Divine in connection with the creation; also called the *Tri-murti*

*Brahman:* the Absolute Being, omnipresent and transcendent

*brahmavidya:* the knowledge of Brahman, the highest wisdom

*darshan:* a blessed seeing sought by a devotee visiting a holy man, a temple, or a holy place

*dharamshalas:* caravanserais (home or shelter for caravans)

*dharma:* cosmic and moral law; "religion," including rules of living and religious rites

*dhoti:* male garment, covering the lower part of the body (Hindi)

*diksha:* initiation

*dvandva:* pair of opposites

*eidos:* form, idea (Greek)

*ekam eva advitiyam:* "One alone and without a second," definition of the Absolute

*eschaton:* in biblical theology the final consummation of the universe when Christ comes again in glory (Greek)

*esseulement:* solitude (French)

*gopis:* cowgirls, the female devotees of Krishna

*guha:* cave, the secret place of the heart, the cave of the heart

**guru:** spiritual master

**Ishvara:** Lord, God

*jivanmukti:* liberation during one's lifetime

*jnana:* wisdom, the true knowledge

*jnani:* a sage, one who has awakened to reality

*karma:* action, work, the result of acts done in a previous life

*keshi:* acosmic ascetic of the Vedas, sometimes known as "the hairy ones"

*kevala:* applied to one who has attained unity in total isolation; Abhishiktananda also called it "the solitude that has no name"

**Krishna:** the cowherd God, incarnation of Vishnu

*kshatriya:* the second highest of the four main Hindu castes: the royal or warrior caste

*linga:* the phallic symbol of Shiva everywhere venerated

*mahāvākyas:* the great words or mystical phrases of the Upanishads, such as "I am Brahman," "Thou art That"

**mantra:** a formula of prayer or invocation

*mahaprasthana:* the great departure; death

*maya:* the undefinable condition of the world of manifestation, which cannot be called real or unreal

*mrityu:* Death

*mukti:* final liberation

*muni:* an ascetic vowed to silence

*murti:* image, manifestation, idols in temples

*namajapa:* the prayer of the Name

**Nataraja:** the king of the Dance, one of the names and one manifestation of Shiva in his cosmic dance

*neti-neti:* not this, not that

**OM, AUM:** the sacred syllable; means also "so be it" (cf. *amen*)

*Parama-atman:* the supreme Self, God

*pleroma:* fullness (Greek)

*purnam:* fullness

**Purusha:** Man; the archetypal, primordial Man; the inner person or the Spirit

*rishis:* Vedic seers

*Saccidananda:* a combination of three Sanskrit words: *Sat* (being), *Cit* (awareness), *Ananda* (bliss)

*sad-guru:* the true guru, master

*sadhu:* a wandering monk, an ascetic

*saguna:* the Absolute with attributes, God manifested

*sahaja:* an inborn, natural condition

*samadhi:* state of total absorption; ecstasy; also the tomb of a saint

*samatva:* inner equilibrium

*sanatana dharma:* the eternal law; the traditional name of the religion derived from the Vedas, commonly called Hinduism

*sandhya:* junction, meeting; especially the "conjunctions" of day and night at sunset or sunrise

*sannyasa:* the life of total renunciation

*sannyasi:* renouncer, a Hindu monk

*satori:* illumination, realization in Zen (Japanese)

*satyam:* truth, reality

# Glossary

***Shakti:*** force, power, energy; the active power of God manifested through the universe, often personified as a feminine principle

***Shivalinga:*** a form of the formless Shiva

*sunyata:* emptiness, the void

*tat tvam asi:* Thou art That

*tavam:* asceticism and the merit acquired by asceticism (Tamil)

*tundu:* a strip of cloth thrown over the shoulder (Tamil)

*upadesha:* spiritual teaching; instruction

**Veda:** knowledge, science; name given to the revealed scriptures of Hinduism.

*yajna:* ritual sacrifice

# Introduction

*Brittany*

Swami Abhishiktananda would have been seen at any time as a remarkable man, for he was uncompromising, passionate, bold, eloquent, and fearless. So what puts this Breton-born country boy among the most significant spiritual figures of the twentieth century, deserving a place in a series called "Modern Spiritual Masters"? He has earned it for the courage with which he endured the anguish of being torn between two great religious traditions, for the radiance that emanated from him after his great "awakening" experience and for his legacy of diaries, books, and letters, which confirm that he was not only a pioneer in interfaith relations, but a mystic on a par with Meister Eckhart, St. John of the Cross, Ramana Maharshi, and the Dalai Lama.

The story of Abhishiktananda is a story of transformation. It tells how Henri Le Saux, the eldest son of a large, devoutly Roman Catholic family, became a Benedictine monk who was taken over by a passionate longing to go to India. In 1948 he achieved his ambition: the monk became a *sannyasi,* and Dom Henri became Swami Abhishiktananda. He co-founded Shantivanam, an ashram in Tamil Nadu, and after many years of travel and exploration of India spent the last years of his life living as a hermit in a hut in the high Himalayas. So the devout Roman Catholic struggled with the enchantment of Hinduism and the Benedictine monk, initially a typical product of French Catholicism before the Second Vatican Council, found himself at the cutting edge of twentieth-century spirituality. It is the story of a man searching for God, prepared to give up everything and to risk all in the search. A man caught in contradiction but ultimately finding reconciliation in the truth beyond the opposites.

He was born Henri Le Saux in 1910 in St. Briac, a little town in the north of France, in Brittany. His parents ran a grocery shop and were devout Roman Catholics, very French — indeed very Breton. Henri was the eldest by seven years, thus becoming almost a second father to his siblings and developing a special, very deep, relationship with his mother — after all he had her to himself for nearly eight years. He was also a practical man, which somehow one does not expect but which perhaps owes something to his place in the family.

He was a brilliant student, and in 1929 he became a Benedictine monk at the monastery of Kergonan in south Brittany. He did this completely wholeheartedly, writing very typically that "a monk cannot accept mediocrity; only extremes are appropriate for him."[1] He was not a man for half measures, and already he felt that God asked for everything. He was, as a great friend said of him, "madly in love with God."

His monastic routine was interrupted when he did his military service and again in 1940 when general mobilization was decreed and he served as a foot soldier. He was captured in the Mayenne when his unit was surrounded by German troops. He managed to escape before the names were taken, and he somehow contrived to borrow a bike and rode home to St. Briac: his practical streak proved useful.

On his return to the monastery he was made *cérémonaire*, the monk in charge of the liturgy, one of the most important jobs in the monastery. Even in those days when liturgy was strict, he was considered an exceptionally punctilious liturgist. When we see how he developed in his long years in India, this has a

---

1. To Raymond Macé, October 27, 1929, *Life*, 6.

comic side to it — he himself would laugh when he remembered the way he insisted that everything was done "Just so. Spick and span." Despite this fussiness and strictness he was very popular with the monks because he did everything in such a kind and friendly way. He was also librarian and taught church history and patristics.

He was a good and devoted monk, and it must have been assumed that he would see out his days in the monastery of Kergonan. However — unknown to absolutely everyone, the monks, his abbot, even his devoted family — he had become obsessed with the idea that he must go to India. This can be dated with some accuracy to 1934, when he was only twenty-four years old and even before he was ordained. How he acquired this passion to go to India has an intriguing element of mystery in it, as it seems that a few articles in magazines sent to Kergonan by a Belgian monastery were the only possible source of his interest. His friend Canon Lemarié, with whom he corresponded all his life, was mystified too, as there was little on the subject in the library at Kergonan and certainly none of the great scriptures such as the Upanishads or the Bhagavad Gita. At most there were a few reviews of the missions to the East.

Henri's attitude to his monastery was ambivalent. On the one hand he had taken a vow of stability, requiring him to remain in his monastery for the rest of his life; also he loved Kergonan, only weeks before his death admitting that Kergonan had been the background of all that he had been able to do in later life. On the other hand there were times when the negative side could not be contained, and he admitted to a distaste for the monastery and conceded that life in the monastery did not fulfill him; indeed that "it was in my deep dissatisfaction that my desire to come to India was born."[2]

---

2. Ibid., March 13, 1967, *Life*, 13.

There is no certainty as to what drew him to India, though there is the possible influence of a missionary uncle, who the family had been encouraged to think died a martyr's death and was thus an inspiration to the young Henri. Somehow the air of mystery adds to the force of his passion: it seems so unreasonable, based on so little direct information, that it was as if there was something in his blood that he simply could not deny. This feeling is reinforced by the determination he showed in actually getting there at a time when the passage to India was not the well-worn route it has now become. His efforts started immediately after the death of his beloved mother; he would not have left France while she was alive. He went to see his abbot, explaining that he wanted to go to India to establish the contemplative monastic life there in an Indian form; or if that was not possible at least to live in India as a hermit.

For four years he wrote letters to likely people in India, endured disappointments, vacillations, hesitancy, and the changing of ecclesiastical minds. He persisted, and at last, on July 26, 1948, he left a sad monastic community behind him, for he was a popular monk, and set sail for India — the fulfillment of a dream that had had him in its grip for fourteen years. He was never to return to France.

## *India*

He arrived in India in August 1948, a year after Independence and six months after the assassination of Gandhi, though curiously he writes little about these momentous events. He joined Father Monchanin, an extraordinary and brilliant French diocesan priest who had been living in India for some time; in 1951 the ashram for which they both longed, which they called Shantivanam, Forest of Peace, was inaugurated, and they both took Indian names, Henri Le Saux becoming Abhishiktananda ("the Bliss of the Anointed One"). He wanted Indian monasticism to be firmly established on a well-tested Rule, and to take its inspiration from the best products of Western monasticism. In other words he wanted to Christianize India along Benedictine lines. How he was to change!

For the next eighteen years he lived in Shantivanam — or perhaps it would be truer to say that Shantivanam was his base, for he spent much of his time wandering around India, wanting to experience the country and its spirituality for himself; he was not content to read about it or even just to talk about it. In everything Abhishiktananda did while he was in India, the desire for firsthand experience rather than for simply theoretical understanding is central.

He had, it might seem, achieved his ambition. He had traveled to India, met a like-minded colleague, and founded an ashram. But this, it turned out, was not to be where his real calling lay. It is not clear exactly when he started losing interest in Shantivanam, but lose interest he most certainly did. Somehow the spark does not really seem to have been lit, even in the early days. This was partly due to problems in his relationship with Father Monchanin, for instance, that Abhishiktananda resented having to do all the practical work. But Monchanin was in poor health and impractical by nature, so one can see the difficulties for him too. The real cause of his loss of interest lay elsewhere: he had only been in India for a few months when something happened that was to affect the rest of his life and, more immediately, affect his attitude to Shantivanam. He went to Tiruvannamalai, to the Holy Mountain of Arunachala, where the great sage Ramana Maharshi lived.

## *Ramana Maharshi*

Meeting Ramana Maharshi was perhaps the most important moment of his life so far. Ramana taught mainly through silence, seeking what he called "Awakening." When pressed he would constantly ask the question "Who am I? What is the Self?" Sometimes he would answer his own question by saying, "The Self is only Be-ing, not being this or that. It is simply Being." Though Ramana's writings had not been translated into French at the time, Abhishiktananda had read enough about him in articles in various periodicals to think that his visit to the famous sage was going to be a high point in his life.

It was 1949. Ramana was seventy when Abhishiktananda and Monchanin went to see him, and very frail after a life of asceticism. Abhishiktananda was convinced that something was going to take place between them, that he would receive a message, if not in words, at least that something would be communicated spiritually. But there is nothing so destructive of fulfillment as high expectation. Nothing happened. He felt let down and filled with sadness. He did not even like the context in which he met the sage — the liturgical atmosphere, the constant reference to him as "Bhagavan," which, as it means "Lord," he considered almost blasphemous when applied to a human being. All he could see was an old man with a gentle face and beautiful eyes. So ordinary, rather like his own grandfather. All through the meal which followed the *darshan*, Abhishiktananda could not take his eyes off him. He watched him eat the same food as they did, use his fingers just as they did, occasionally talk as they did. But how could he accept being called "Bhagavan"? Why did he allow himself to be worshiped in this way? Where was the halo? Ironically, in view of the importance Ramana was to have in his life, this first meeting was a huge disappointment.

That evening, for the first time, Abhishiktananda heard the Vedas chanted, as timelessly and simply as they had been chanted by the *rishis* in the forests for thousands of years. These archetypal sounds drew him as nothing so far had done. Something was stirring, though he did not yet know what it was or how to express it.

Six months later he returned to Tiruvannamalai, now released from his Western clothes and comfortable in *kavi*, the two strips of orange cloth worn by Hindu ascetics, only to find Ramana very ill with a cancerous tumor on his arm and unable to see anyone but his medical helpers and closest friends. However, he was able to stay at the ashram, and during his time there Ramana began to hold *darshan* again, Abhishiktananda doing his best to keep his rational mind in abeyance and trying "simply to attend to the hidden influence."

He spent some time wandering around the caves hewed into the side of the mountain; he talked to Ramana's disciples and learned more about the sage he was coming to venerate so deeply. He came to realize that at Arunachala there was not only a great sage, but a temple and, most of all, a mountain — Arunachala itself; grace could be bestowed through any of these three channels. This was not yet part of his experience, but one day it would be the mountain itself which would draw him, as it had drawn Ramana himself.

Yet it was two and a half years before he returned to Tiruvannamalai, and by then Ramana had died. The Vedas were chanted at his tomb and once again Abhishiktananda fell under their spell. He also discovered that there were hermitages scattered around the mountainside and a brahmin, who looked after the visitors, told Abhishiktananda that there was an empty cave overlooking the Temple and that he was welcome to settle there. He began to understand. "If Ramana was himself so great, how much more so must be this Arunachala which drew Ramana to himself?"[3]

It was is if Abhishiktananda had fallen in love with the mountain:

> It is all up with anyone who has paused, even for a moment, to attend to the gentle whisper of Arunachala.

---

3. *Secret*, 23.

Arunachala has already taken him captive, and will play with him without mercy to the bitter end. Darkness after light, desertion after embraces, he will never let him go until he has emptied him of everything in himself that is not the one and only Arunachala and that still persists in giving him a name, as one names *another* — until he has been finally swallowed up, having disappeared forever in the shining of his Dawn-light, *Aruna*.[4]

The italicized *another* is the only sign he gives of the oneness, the unity, that was to be his goal for the rest of his life. Arunachala was beginning to show him that *another* is not possible, for there is only one.

## *Arunachala*

So at the end of March 1952, this European Benedictine monk in his early forties, for the first time dressed, ate, and lived as a *sadhu*, a wandering monk, in the caves of Arunachala. The fact that he also lived in silence he attributed to the "spell-binding wiles" of the mountain.

His day started early in the morning. While it was still dark, he would say Mass in his cave, deep in the heart of the mountain. Then he would sit in front of his *sacro speco*,[5] as he called his cave, and wait for the sun to rise. As the dawn broke, blazing with the warm redness that gives the mountain its name,[6] he would greet it in the Indian way, hands together about his head, and, making a full prostration, sing the Lumen Christi and the Gloria as they are sung at dawn in the Syrian church. He sang Lauds, saying the Lord's Prayer with his arms stretched out facing Tiruvannamalai, the town at the foot of Arunachala. It is a

---

4. Ibid.
5. *Sacro speco*: "sacred space," as St. Benedict's cave at Subiaco was known.
6. Arunachala: "aruna" — the rosy color of the dawn; "achala" — mountain.

measure of his involvement with the place that the town had already become another word that he prefaced with the personal pronoun — it was now "my" Tiruvannamalai as it was already "my" Hindus and "my" people.

The tension in which he was to live for so long was beginning to make itself felt. He had already admitted to having "two loves" — India and France. Now more divisions were appearing. He was wearing the clothes of a Hindu ascetic and longing to penetrate the spirit of Hinduism, yet he was a French priest, deeply Christian, and of the old-fashioned variety, never traveling without his Mass kit and unable to say Mass unless there was room to stand upright and a door that could be locked to prevent the sacred vessels from being profaned — two conditions not readily found in a cave in a mountainside. Now, as he came to love the mountain, he found a third division, as his heart was becoming divided between the sacred river Kavery, at Shantivanam where he lived with Father Monchanin, and the sacred mountain of Arunachala, home of Ramana Maharshi.

## *Experience*

In his determination to live everything from experience rather than theory Abhishiktananda immersed himself totally in Hinduism. He lived as the poorest of the poor, always traveled third class, went on pilgrimages, climbed to the sources of the Ganges, braved his European embarrassment and took a begging bowl for a little rice and worshiped with people of other faiths at a time when this was not only unusual but could also risk his standing as a Christian monk. He met people of all nationalities and faiths, spent periods of total solitude, celebrated Mass sitting cross-legged on the banks of the Ganges, and followed teachings unacceptable to most orthodox Christians in the 1950s. He dived into the experience of Hinduism and swam in its waters with a joy tempered only by constant worry that he was being untrue to his Christianity.

One of the ways in which his openness to the Hindu experience was most remarkable was in his search for a teacher. Apart from Ramana Maharshi, from whom he first learned about the advaitic tradition that was to have such an influence on his life, there were three men who influenced him particularly. One he met at Arunachala and usually referred to him by his first name, Harilal. His full name was H. W. L. Poonja. He was a brahmin from Punjab, a disciple of Ramana Maharshi, and a strict advaitin; in his working life he was the manager of iron and manganese mines in the jungles of Mysore and was a married man with a family. While from Abhishiktananda's point of view it was a providential meeting, Harilal himself had set about finding the Frenchman quite deliberately. He had passed him one morning in the bazaar, and seeing into the Frenchman's eyes was immediately convinced that this was someone he had to meet. So he persuaded a local Tamil to take him to Abhishiktananda's cave on the side of the Holy Mountain.

Abhishiktananda could not understand how anyone had found him; he had thought he was hidden from the world. "You called me," said Harilal, "and here I am...the Self attracts the Self. What else do you expect?"[7] This unusual introduction set the tone for a relationship, not the relationship of a disciple to his guru; it was more the friendship of two souls, with one, at the moment, more advanced. It was precisely what Abhishiktananda needed at this moment in his life, and the relationship was to resonate through the next years.

Harilal never minced his words, and he started as he had every intention of going on, with a severe reprimand. It was caused by Abhishiktananda, with his usual ability to laugh at

---

7. *Secret*, 81.

himself, admitting that he liked to quote from the Bhagavad-Gita and the Upanishads as he found it impressed people. He was about to quote a text, adding — might one guess with a self-conscious casualness? — that he had learned a little Sanskrit, when Harilal interrupted: "And what is the use of all that? All your books, all the time lost in learning different languages! Which language do you use to converse with the *atman*?... The *atman* has nothing to do either with books, or with languages, or with any scripture whatever. *It is* — and that's all."[8] He went on to say that only in the ultimate silence is the *atman* revealed. He was convinced that Abhishiktananda was very close to the true awakening experience, but the demands upon him were huge. It was not only books that had to go; even harder sacrifices were needed:

> There is only one thing you need, and that is to break the last bonds that are holding you back. You are quite ready for it. Leave off your prayers, your worship. Your contemplation of this or that. Realize that *you are*, *tat tvam asi* — you are That![9]

It was as if Abhishiktananda had been stripped of everything. He had given up his country, his family, marriage, any sort of financial security, and most physical comforts. He already spent weeks in solitude and silence. Now he was being asked to give up his beloved books and, even worse, his Christian identity and worship. The way of experience is hard.

He was poised on the edge of an abyss as he tried to reconcile Christianity and *advaita*, desperately in need of help. He found it in a Parsi doctor who had attended Mahatma Gandhi — Dr. Dinshaw Mehta. He could not accept Dr. Mehta's teaching totally, particularly the way in which he wanted to encourage

---

8. Ibid., 82.
9. Ibid., 84.

his devotion to Christ, but not the Christ of the church. It is a measure of Abhishiktananda's humility as well as of his desperate need for help that he tried so hard to learn from him. This was for him a great lesson in surrender. In fact Dr. Mehta was one of those who advised him to spend a month in complete solitude. This was a solitude even greater than the solitude he had experienced in the caves of Arunachala; he did not even see the hands of the silent messenger who delivered his food through a revolving hatch. It was a grueling time for him with periods when his spiritual strings were tuned to a pitch almost beyond his bearing. Yet when it ended he dreaded the thought of leaving, and on the last day, when he said Mass and opened the door that had been shut for thirty-two days, he burst into tears. He had only one wish, to return to the solitude and the silence.

## *At the Feet of a Guru*

The other person who had advised this period of total solitude was Sri Gnanananda, a famous guru, believed to be 120 years old and known as the holy man of Tirukoyilur. To be true to his desire to live everything at the level of experience Abhishiktananda, Benedictine monk though he was, sought God in the way of the Hindu — through a guru. He knew that sometimes divine grace simply descends, without explanation, nor did he discount the value of intelligent and careful reading of scripture. But he was already so deeply immersed in India that the way to realization for him meant to follow the Indian tradition and learn from the lips of those who had trodden the path and knew its joys and dangers for themselves.

The relationship of the guru and the disciple is much misunderstood in the West and so is rejected, even sometimes mocked. At its best and purest this is a truly wonderful relationship whose aim is to impart the highest knowledge and understanding. Most importantly the guru knows, as is said in the Katha Upanishad, that the disciple "cannot be taught by one who has not reached him; and he cannot be reached by much thinking. The way to him is through a Teacher who has seen him."[10] The one who becomes a guru is one who speaks only from experience. Then if the disciple comes, an extraordinary bond can develop between them. Now Abhishiktananda could joke to his family, "I have become a real Hindu monk!"[11] and, more seriously, write that "there is in the Gospel much more than Christian piety has ever discovered."

These meetings with his guru had led Abhishiktananda closer to the heart of *advaita*, but far from being radiant with peace and optimism, he was torn apart by conflict; he still could not reconcile the advaitic path with the Christianity that was so deep in his heart.

Ramana Maharshi had been the catalyst for Abhishiktananda's search for awakening. He had been shaken by his encounter with Harilal, he had learned from Dr. Mehta, and most of all he had been enriched by finding a guru. The next steps had to be taken on his own. He was to have many friends, even some to whom he could talk freely, but no one else took the role of teacher or guru in his life.

## A Very Active Hermit

Abhishiktananda was to live another twenty years, all of them spent in India. He never returned to France or went anywhere else — all that time he was working out the implications of his experiences, most of all trying to reconcile the Christian faith from which he never wavered with the bliss and peace of *advaita*. He once wrote, "I am like someone who has one foot on one side of the gulf, and the other on the other side. I would

---

10. *The Upanishads*, trans. Juan Mascaro (New York: Penguin Books, 1965), 58.
11. MT, March 25, 1956, *Life*, 106.

like to throw a bridge across, but do not know where to fasten it, the walls are so smooth."[12] And all the time he was seeking true enlightenment, the final awakening which he knew was there but which eluded him for so long. Abhishiktananda's real story is in this inner struggle, but though by now he was in almost every way a *sannyasi*, living a life of total renunciation, he also had an eventful outer life, traveling widely over India.

In 1959 he went to the Himalayas for the first time, writing memorably, "Here more than anywhere I am strongly tempted to pitch my tent!"[13] On the way he stayed at Jyotiniketan ashram, where he met Murray Rogers and his community — a friendship that was to be deeply important to all of them. He made numerous other friends, wrote twelve books, many articles, and thousands of letters. Perhaps the most remarkable part of this written legacy is his *Spiritual Diary*, where, through these highly personal, sometimes daily accounts of the intense struggles he endured, we can hear the voice of his pain, the contradictions and tensions he endured, and, sometimes, the joy. Some of these diary entries are hard to understand. They were not, of course, written for publication, and it is hoped that the passages that have been chosen in the following selection will prove a welcome introduction to those who are not familiar with them. They must be some of the most remarkable pieces of spiritual autobiography ever written.

His books fall into two main categories — the experiential and the theoretical. *In Guru and Disciple, The Mountain of the Lord*, and *The Secret of Arunachala* he wrote about experiences and events in his life in India — of meeting Sri Gnanananda, of making a pilgrimage to one of the sources of the Ganges, and of meeting Ramana Maharshi at Arunachala. These books are true accounts of his experiences, and he did not seem to have wished

---

12. To his family, December 26, 1951, *Life*, 56.
13. To Canon Lemarié, March 18, 1961, *Life*, 151.

a word in them unwritten. His reaction to the other books was more complicated, for he grew and changed so much and so fast that sometimes his feelings changed about a book between his writing of it and its publication. The book considered one his greatest, *Saccidananda,* falls, by his own admission, into this category. There is no recorded evidence of his reaction to his best-known book, *Prayer,* or to the beautiful essays in *The Further Shore,* which were not published until after his death. He was also an animated and frequent letter writer; the collection made by James Stuart, *Swami Abhishiktananda: His Life Told through His Letters,* along with his spiritual diary, *Ascent to the Depth of the Heart,* are a source of endless insights into his extraordinary spiritual journey.

Increasingly Abhishiktananda was asked to speak at conferences and to direct retreats. He only rarely accepted, though he did attend theological conferences held at Shantivanam, Jyotiniketan, Bangalore, and Bombay. In the early 1960s he was involved with a series of ecumenical meetings organized by Dr. Jacques-Albert Cuttat, then the Swiss ambassador to India. Abhishiktananda was the animator and this was the intellectual background against which much of his thought at the time was worked out and which is the basis of his book *Hindu-Christian Meeting Point.*

In 1961 he attended the meeting of the World Council of Churches in Delhi, the welcome he received giving a boost to his always rather tenuous hold on confidence; he felt it was a measure of the extent to which he and his ideas were becoming accepted by the church. He frequently, however, criticized the institution, longing, for instance, for it to be "spiritually radiant" and lamenting that "the church has given so much evidence of worldliness that its spiritual and contemplative character has often almost disappeared from sight."[14] It was

---

14. BB, September 16, 1966, *LS&T,* 153.

very important to him to be accepted as a Christian, and the occasions when his Christianity was doubted were deeply distressing to him. He longed for the Western church to establish what he called "centers of non-duality" and felt that "we are approaching a real nuclear explosion in the sphere of religion." Nor did the thought of this worry him too much. Towards the end of his life he wrote. "The structures will blow up, but what does it matter? There are plenty of tracks leading to the summit of Arunachala!"[15] Perhaps if those in charge of the direction the church was taking had understood his analogy between the church and the Holy Mountain, he would have been more optimistic.

## *Gyansu*

In 1968 Abhishiktananda at last did something that had been in his mind for some time. He moved to a place where he hoped that nothing would distract him from the one essential, his longing for "Being there, simply."[16] Gyansu is near Uttarkashi, north of Rishikesh on the pilgrimage route to Gangotri. His *kutiya*, his hut, was one of ten little houses built for *sadhus,* close to the bank of the river; it was essentially a one-roomed house, the Ganga thundering past only three or four yards away. It was built of stones covered with mud plaster, with large untrimmed slates, carried down from the mountainside, for a roof. The main room was filled with the books and papers that accompanied him everywhere, there were a few necessities like a lantern, essential for the dark lonely nights, a screw driver, and a hammer — remember Abhishiktananda was a practical man, quite capable of putting things to rights himself — and basic supplies such as flour, rice, and dhal. There

---

15. Letter to MC, January 28, 1972, *LS&T,* 157.
16. Letter to MC, October 4, 1971, *LS&T,* 353.

was a tiny lean-to kitchen and a cell made of bamboo matting, which, with the addition of a *charpoy,* a string bed, doubled as spare room and study. The walls of this little room were so full of holes that to keep out the draft Abhishiktananda had filled them with rolled-up pages of *Informations Catholiques,* stuffing them in with a screwdriver. Up a rickety ladder was a small attic room that acted as both box room and chapel. It was, as one of the few friends permitted to visit him there said, "wonderfully Heath Robinson."*

In October 1968, soon after the ambivalent sadness of his departure from Shantivanam, he settled in his *kutiya,* firmly believing that this would be his home, though as so often he was caught between those people who told him never to move from Gyansu and those who insisted he make an exception to go and see them — and of course *only* them. The contradictory advice of these friends echoed his own ambivalence, but for the rest of his life he did manage to stay at Gyansu for at least half the year. There he found nothing distracted him from the essential; there, and he once said there *only,* he felt fully alive. Soon he made it not only a retreat but a home, as he planted fruit trees and vegetables — beans, marrows, cucumbers, pumpkins. For lunch he would mostly have rice, split peas, potatoes, and marrow and at first he also allowed himself half a liter of milk a day, something which he later gave up so that he could save the money and send it to some poor people he had supported for many years.

## Marc Chaduc

His main reason for leaving Gyansu from time to time was to go and see friends and the few disciples who were beginning to be

---

*Heath Robinson was a cartoonist, whose crazy inventions captured the public imagination in the UK in the first half of the twentieth century. – Ed.

an important part of his life. Most important of all was a young Frenchman he met in 1971 named Marc Chaduc, who became his disciple and took the name of Ajatananda — "the joy of the never born." Marc arrived in India on October 21, 1971, and Abhishiktananda's life underwent a revolutionary change, reaching a peak of fulfillment he had never before experienced. The young seminarian and the sixty-one-year-old French *sadhu* quickly found they were living the fullness of the guru-disciple relationship. The disciple was ready for his guru and Abhishiktananda was ready for him. "Guru and disciple are a dyad, a pair, whose two components call for each other and belong together. No more than the two poles (of a magnet) can they exist without being related to each other."[17] He had experienced one side of this extraordinary relationship between guru and disciple; he was about to experience the other.

It is hard for Westerners to understand the relationship that developed between Marc and Abhishiktananda. It was as if there was only one "I," *advaita* experienced by these two people at the same time. It was a relationship of total love yet of total non-attachment, the communion between guru and disciple taking place at the very center of the self, drawing on experience springing from the deepest level of being. Later he wrote to Marc that he remained incapable of understanding what had happened: "This non-dual dyad of which I spoke in Gnanananda, we have lived out with such intensity. In discovering you as son, I have found myself."[18] It had become a relationship of which Abhishiktananda wrote: "I am now following you (on your way); or better, I am you here, and you are I there." Now Abhishiktananda knew, without a shadow of doubt, that he had found "a true total disciple." He was very aware of the responsibility he carried and was frightened by it,

---

17. *Guru*, 28–29.
18. Quoted in Odette Bauman-Despeigne, "The Spiritual Way of Henri Le Saux, Swami Abhishiktananda," *La Vie Spirituelle* 691 (September–October 1990): 22.

wondering if he was handling Marc well, nervous that perhaps he was not.

## *Illness and Death*

It was probably partly the fact that he was living so intensely in this relationship with Marc that on July 14, 1973, Abhishiktananda had a heart attack. He described this as the greatest moment of his life — the moment when he really understood. He was in a street in Rishikesh when it happened, and it was his highest spiritual experience. He was transformed. It was the moment when the lightning struck him, and he died to everything as never before. The mist fell from his eyes, and he was able to answer the question he had asked ever since that day nearly twenty-five years earlier when he had first asked, "Who am I?"

Five months later, on December 7, 1973, he died.

Abhishiktananda became less and less interested in trying to found anything or form anything. He became content not even to know where he was going. He was a real nomad, always on the move, not belonging anywhere. Shantivanam, his hut in the Himalayas, the nursing home at Indore where he stayed on many occasions and where he died — all were bases from which to wander. He would never settle down; he was hungry for the "beyond." For many years he wasn't a man of peace, but a man living through extreme tensions. He knew *advaita* — non-duality — was true. He loved and believed in Christ and was seriously threatened by people who doubted that he was a real Christian, shaken to the core if anyone doubted his orthodoxy. He wanted Roman Catholics to know he was a real Roman Catholic. How could he reconcile the two? That was the great tension of much of his life, causing him real anguish and suffering.

He remained a priest, and he remained a Benedictine monk, but he was a long way from the average expectations of a Catholic priest. He was beyond all structures, yet he remained a disciple of Jesus. As far as the church is concerned, he never left it but he did become distanced from it. He came to see more and more clearly the false duality of the church, for instance, in regarding people as active *or* contemplative. In the end even the Mass became unimportant: he could celebrate or not. Everything was divine, so it didn't really matter. But when he did say Mass, it was a momentous occasion, for he was at the level of knowing beyond any words.

The only distinction he would make was between being and doing. In all other ways he couldn't make distinctions: he couldn't insist on keeping Christianity separate and on top; he couldn't claim that Christian mysticism took people further. Duality simply didn't exist for him. Most of all he wanted simply to be. As he wrote to Raimon Panikkar: "To do? To do what? I am not here to do anything, but to be."

By the end of his life he was widely perceived as a holy man, an enlightened being. A Japanese Dominican monk who became a close friend wrote of an occasion when his "double-belongingness" was transcended as his inborn French Catholicism met his beloved Hinduism. They were celebrating Bara Din, as the great feast of the Nativity is known in India. A Catholic girl began to sing a Gregorian chant of the feast, accompanied by one of the Hindus. It was too much for Abhishiktananda, who for twenty-five years had cut himself off from his motherland and his monastic brothers: "Stop, please stop," he cried out explosively. "It's tearing me apart." At this point the two traditions must have met in Abhishiktananda as never before, for a Hindu friend, his eyes on Abhishiktananda, said, "Christ is here. I am looking at him."

So was he, as has been suggested, "a weird and crazy monk," or was he a man who, in his courage in enduring the anguish of being split between two great traditions, reached unusual heights of spiritual greatness and who, over thirty years after his death, is a beacon to those striving to remain faithful to one tradition while being open to the truths of others? He was, in fact, a Christian for today, able to transcend differences between religions and live in the transcendent truth.

# Swami Abhishiktananda

ॐ

# 1

# Benedictine Monk

ॐ

*Despite the long years that Abhishiktananda was to spend in India, he remained feeling, as he put it, "terribly, terribly French." Just how much France meant to him is shown in a letter written toward the end of his life to a compatriot, originally from the west coast of Brittany, who had settled in New York.*

## BRITTANY

OM. At noon a letter from you from Brittany. I cannot resist writing to you there at once. You make me dream, relive those things which I usually push into the background in order to be able to live my life in peace. How aptly you said that after twenty years you slipped back at once like a snake into its old skin. It seems only yesterday that we were ten, eleven years old — that wonderful age! And everything else seems to have overlaid it, like a cloak that you have put on for a long journey.... Perhaps behind all the high-sounding reasons that I give for refusing and arguing against any possibility of returning there, is my fear of not being able to bear it emotionally, and the great difficulty I would have afterwards in taking up my "role" again.

I have found on the map of Finistère in my old 1924 Larousse ... your village deep in a little cove.... St. Guénolé, Locquénolé, names which make me dream. I do not know Finistère; I am from St. Malo and Cap Fréhel, also deep in a cove.... The Himalayas are splendid, and Arunachala is greater still; yet what can be compared to the sea of my Emerald Coast (not blue as a jay's wing, like yours)? All this belongs to the depth of my being. It is like those Tridentine Masses and the Gregorian chant of the monasteries, which I would doubtless put on again like a glove, even after having lived the marvelous experience of "spontaneous" Masses or of those Masses in the Upanishadic tradition which I celebrate each morning and which help me to carry on.... To pass from Manhattan to the moors of St. Guénolé is probably as rude a shock as to pass from the Himalayas to a monastery on the moors of Carnac; and that is why I "feel" so much all that your letter conveys.... Write again soon, I feel you so much closer in our Brittany. At least I can imagine it to some extent, despite the immense changes since the war; whereas for me New York and America are at a "lunar" distance, and I guess that if I ever got there I should be *flattened* like some of the cosmonauts.

Before I send this off, a deep bow to the ocean for me, please!
— AMS, August 3, 1971, *Life*, 10–11

*Abhishiktananda was a man in the grip of vocational callings — first to be a Benedictine monk, then to go to India, finally to be a hermit. But ultimately it was God himself he sought.*

## VOCATION

What has drawn me from the beginning, and what still leads me on, is the hope of finding there the presence of God more immediately than anywhere else. I have a very ambitious spirit — and this is permissible, is it not? when it is a matter of seeking God — and I hope I shall not be disappointed.
— To the Novice Master, December 4, 1928, *Life*, 3

A monk cannot accept mediocrity; only extremes are appropriate for him. — RM, October 27, 1929, *Life*, 6

There is the call to remain in the cave, and there are the calls which come to you from outside, and the Spirit weaves its way through both kinds. — TL, February 16, 1967, *Life*, 213

You sometimes tell me that my life is so difficult to understand. In fact, it was hardly my own choice, it has landed on me from above, day after day, year after year. And truly it is marvelous. If at least I could pass on to the Christian world the honey which I gather in the Hindu world, and vice versa, however dislocating it may sometimes be.
— AG, April 18, 1969, *Life*, 237–38

It would be a betrayal of all that I stand for, solitude, silence, and monastic poverty; I have no more sought solitude than Amos sought the role of a prophet, but once placed in that position, nothing else remains for me but to be a hermit for good, and not a mere salesman of solitude and monastic life.
— RP, December 11, 1969, *Life*, 250

Beyond, always beyond! It is not your gifts, Lord, that I desire, but yourself... — Typescript 108, ALA, quoted in *Life*, 9

## LETTER TO LOUISETTE

*Abhishiktananda, who was of course born Henri Le Saux, was devoted to his family. This letter to his sister Louise, who had lost her first husband, Marcel, in the war, was written soon after the death of his beloved mother. It reflects a close and devout Catholic family, Henri already a Benedictine monk and his sister Annette considering entering a convent.*

> Abbaye Sainte Anne de Kergonan
> Wednesday evening, 31st Jan. 1945.

My little Louisette

So, you're worrying again about India. However, I told you quite clearly the other day what it was all about. It is a dream and a much cherished dream, but everything points to its never being anything more than a dream. So don't worry about it. Sufficient unto each day is the evil thereof.

As for Annette, everyone must take their part seriously as to her missionary and religious vocation. When the Good Lord calls in this way and blesses a family like this, one must have enough faith to give him thanks. Maman suffered greatly, too, to see me wanting to become a monk; she accepted it and made the sacrifice. There's no question of holding back with the Good Lord. When the Good Lord asks of someone the gift of his or her life, you must understand that he is everything, and worthy of being given all, no question of bargaining, of calculating how to taste a little freedom, of doing one's bit and the rest. He is generous and we are not. For an unmarried person who wants to consecrate his or her life to God, there is normally only one way, the religious life. The rest is fantasy. Otherwise you ruin your life, you ruin your apostolic mission and prepare yourself for a less lovely heaven. Tell me, what does a little pain count for in the face of the love one owes to the Good Lord who has loved us so much and loves us so much.... Perhaps that's hard. That is not what it is about. Maman's example showed us that one is not on earth to play. We are on earth to love the Good Lord, to respond a little to the love that he has offered us. The ordeals are a means of making that love easier for us. I have already written it several times: is it not true that we all love the Good Lord a little, if not a great deal, more than a year ago?

It is a severe directive, I know. But it is necessary to give it. My poor little sister, I feel that all this must be painful for you. But you can carry it now; you gained much strength last year.

The Good Lord helped you greatly and has given you much. When we see each other, we will talk about it out loud. Oh we must absolutely manage to see each other privately, as Marie Thérèse says. In any case, don't worry ahead of time, not about this either. It will be at least two or three years before Annette becomes a nun and a few years more before she leaves France. In the meantime, live again all your memories since you have them with you. I can hardly think myself, without risking giving it up, and I am incapable of having a photo other than in my wallet.

As you said at the end of your letter, my little Louisette, you are much more brave than your letters sometime seem. Maman and Marcel help you. And the Good Lord teaches you to look for and to find in him both strength and consolation. Later, you will understand all these things better.

Work as hard as you can to reduce the business expenditure, get the unions moving, or other things. It could become difficult to get stock, but thanks to the capital, it will always be possible to get what is most urgent. It must be right to plan a summer season, as the Parisians will be eager to refresh themselves with a visit to the sea. You will doubtless be thinking of doing business this month to avoid the extra costs.

For Mass, it will be forty francs from now on. As far as I'm concerned, I'm sure the Good Lord takes as much notice of a Mass asked for by someone poor in need, as a thousand asked for by someone rich. So don't worry too much as to how much. But the important thing is never to stop praying for our dear ones, above all for Marcel. But be sure that our troubles and our sacrifices, bravely accepted, serve to shorten the purgatory of those we love.

My little sister, I would so love to help you more to shoulder your troubles, that I feel so strongly. But you already carry them so well, which gives me great comfort.

With a big hug, Henri
 — To his sister Louisette, January 31, 1945, A. le B. Coll.

*After many years of struggle, Abhishiktananda at last achieved his ambition and was given permission to go to India. He had arranged to join a French priest, Father Jules Monchanin, a highly intellectual man who had chosen to live as a hermit in a village in Tamil Nadu, where he was revered as a saint. This is part of a long letter Abhishiktananda wrote to him as he prepared to leave France.*

## FATHER JULES MONCHANIN

I think it will now be good to put before you the basic principles for realizing our project to which my reading and reflection have led me. I certainly do not want to lay down anything *a priori;* for me a fundamental rule is adaptation to circumstances and submission to reality. I gave my ideas very briefly in my letter of May 15. Here they are now, a little further elaborated. You must tell me what you think of them, and whether they fit in with yours. Above all — and here I am sure we are in complete agreement — there must be total Indianization; however far your ideas about this may go, I am perfectly sure of being in agreement with you. But, in my opinion, our starting point should be the Rule of St. Benedict, for in it we have a monastic tradition which is extremely sound and which would relieve us from having to launch out into the unknown — I mean the actual Rule itself, freed from the adaptations which have sometimes been imposed on it in recent centuries, with its original very flexible and universal spirit. I would like to offer to our dear Tamilians the Rule at the moment of its birth, as it were, so that little by little, with experience as the sole guide, specifically Hindu customs could be grafted onto it.

On this basis, like you, I envisage the tree of monasticism once more flourishing in all its variety, with hermits, solitaries, and mendicants; we have to sanctify the whole contemplative thrust of India and Christianize the monastic institutions through which she expresses the depth of her spirit. And around the monastery — the indispensable center of all these varieties of monastic life, to which brothers called to a more special vocation would return for spiritual refreshment — I foresee the development of a very Hindu adaptation of Benedictine Oblates and Benedictine hospitality, in the form of an ashram where Hindus and Christians would come in search of nourishment for their spiritual life. I think the Rule of St. Benedict is sufficiently flexible, in its depth and marvelous stability, to control all these forms of monastic living — in fact, it has already done so in the greatest periods of its history. I noticed this again quite recently when preparing to give a course on ancient and mediaeval monastic history. Moreover you can easily understand that eighteen years of Benedictine life have made me deeply attached to the "holy Rule," and that I dream of giving our blessed Father new children who will fashion a Christian India, as their elder brothers fashioned a Christian Europe. I have every hope that one day we shall discover together many interesting insights on all this; and am I sure that we shall find ourselves in agreement — your article once more convinces me of this.

I would most particularly like to preserve the non-clerical character of the primitive Rule. The clericalization of monastic life restricted its appeal to, or rather, its capacity to respond to, the contemplative potentialities of the Christian spirit; the Middle Ages had to institute lay brothers who, in spite of the holiness attained by many of them, are only half-monks, lacking in particular the Office in choir which is at the very heart of Benedictine life, or more precisely, of all monastic life in community. If we give a clerical character to the monastery that we envisage, this will minimize its value.... I would like to throw wide open to Hindus the gates of a fully monastic life, to open them to all the many people in India who seem to be touched by the call of mysticism.

The conventual prayer would of course be in Tamil, for it should be the source and choice fruit of the private prayer which will fill the day. At the traditional canonical hours, dividing up the times of work (here again we would only have to apply the Holy Rule), we should have, not an exact replica of the monastic Office, but a wise adaptation of it, based on the Psalms, the scriptural Canticles, with readings from the Bible, the Fathers, and the lives of the saints. And instead of our magnificent but untranslatable hymns, why not adopt specifically Hindu spiritual compositions? St. Gregory the Great told Augustine of Canterbury to preserve for Christ the beautiful temples of idols; could we not preserve for him the beautiful tones inspired in Hindu poets by their deep love for God, even if this is externalized in invocations to Shiva or Kali?

You must be familiar with the experience in China of Père Lebbe, whom I often call the most authentic disciple of St. Benedict in our day. His success, based on the very same principles which I am suggesting, has been remarkable, while other foundations in his neighborhood, where they tried hard to reproduce the European way of life or twentieth-century Benedictinism, are stagnating.

Our lifestyle will certainly be very austere, much more so than is the case in our French monasteries. This will be no problem for me, quite the reverse. As you say — and as de Nobili, Britto, and those who followed their lead did in the past — we must live as *sannyasis,* and the life of *sannyasa* is a Hindu institution which has its own traditional rules to which we should submit. Not indeed that we should set out to compete with Hindu ascetics — on the contrary, as Benedict did long ago, we will have to show the supreme importance of the interior life, and the subordinate place of externals; all the same, there is a minimum to which we must conform, and here again experience alone will be our guide. The Lord will give us the necessary strength. Thank God, I enjoy excellent health, even if the regular life of a monastery has not accustomed me to severe shocks, and my age is quite favorable (I am thirty-seven)... but above all I trust in the Lord. Besides, I expect it will be possible to find a place with a healthy climate, not too extreme....

Monastic life cannot be healthy without serious work — "Idleness is the enemy of the soul," says St. Benedict — and history shows that laziness is a risk faced by all monks, Christian, non-Christian, Western or Eastern. In my view work should be both intellectual and manual, according to the individual aptitudes of the monks. For my own part I much prefer intellectual work, but I think we should also bear in mind brothers who may have a more limited intelligence, but are nonetheless capable of a life of contemplation. In any case the need to support ourselves will probably leave us no option. Gandhi has asked Christian monks to give an example of manual labor. The bishops are asking us for a whole range of intellectual work (books, periodicals, publications, to start with!); and more generally, a rethinking of Christian dogma in Hindu terms, and a Christian reinterpretation of Hindu thought.

The latter task is what most attracts me. Still, whatever work we undertake, I am sure that in accordance with the most healthy monastic tradition it must be kept in its proper place, and not become an end in itself. We do not want to start an agricultural estate, or a center for stockbreeding, or a publishing house, or a university; if the Lord grants this — and he surely will after two or three monastic generations, as he did in Europe — it will be splendid, but that will not be our aim. We are monks, seeking to enter even in this life into the kingdom of God. St. Gregory in his *Life of St. Benedict* (c. 3) has a sentence which for me is the fundamental monastic motto: "Alone in the sight of the supreme Beholder, he lived with himself." All the social usefulness of monasticism (economic, or religious and intellectual), if it is to be kept in its right place, must be a *fruit*, not an end in itself. And our exclusively contemplative aim must be all the more stubbornly defended, because the bishops will need us and our participation will appear supremely useful. We shall have to protect ourselves in the same way as we are having to do just now in France....

However, I, and the brother of whom I have spoken, dream of the day when we will be fully Tamilian, in our dress, in our life and customs, sitting in choir for the psalms in the lotus position — if indeed we ever manage to acquire it! — and taking our meals on banana leaves, seated on the ground.

—JM, August 18, 1947, *Life,* 22

## FULFILLMENT THEOLOGY

*For many years Henri Le Saux held the view generally taken by Catholics at that time, that all religions would find their fullness in Christianity — a position known as "fulfillment theology." It is surprising he was still writing from this point of view after many years in India as Swami Abhishiktananda, this passage being written after his first pilgrimage to the High Himalayas in 1959. However he was soon to change and to become one of those most sensitive to the realization that there is one inexpressible mystery beyond all names and forms, thus clearing the way for many who were drawn to that understanding but who lacked the confidence to accept its truth.*

It was therefore entirely right that Christ himself should also go up to the Himalayas, just as once he went up to Jerusalem and to Calvary; and that he should go there, no longer only in the persons of those who are indeed his own, yet know it not, and who worship him under images and symbols whose final meaning they do not perceive — but now also in the person of those whose forehead has been marked with the sign of the cross and who bear his name written on their hearts; and that in their bodies, weighed down with fatigue, he should offer to the Father the price of man's redemption; that in their eyes, enchanted by the beauty of the peaks, he should express to the Father the radiant joy of the redeemed; and that finally through their eager lips he should refresh his church from marvelous springs of water.... So the Christ would fulfill all symbols and crown all expectations, and at last unite all signs in the Reality which he himself is.

•

For Christ himself is also the God of the heights. Seated on a "mount" he gave the charter of the Gospel to the disciples; on a "mount" he appeared to them in his glory; and finally he led them to a "mount" to give them his last blessing before disappearing from their outward eyes — and this final Transfiguration was even more mysterious than that of Tabor and heralded his ultimate *darshana,* his manifestation in the Spirit at the center of their hearts.

Shortly before his death he had said to those who were looking for him: "When I am lifted up from the earth — first on the cross, and then in the Ascension — I will draw all men to myself."

And at the last, when he comes again, he will appear on the clouds, himself veiled, as scripture says, in that "Cloud" which veiled the summits.

•

Christ is the peak of which every earthly peak is a sign. He is that Height which rises up to heaven itself to lay hold of Being and Life. In his Head he even penetrates the supreme mystery of the Father. The earth below is his footstool — or rather, the solid ground in which his roots are sunk deep within the very stuff of our human nature.

He it is who is the true meaning of the myth of Shiva, practicing austerity in the Himalayas, who received on his head the stream of grace from on high and let it flow down his body upon mankind. He is the Mediator, the One in whom God makes himself known and grants to all the joy of contemplating his very Face.

He is that Column of Light and Fire, celebrated in the myth of Shiva-Arunachala, with one pole penetrating the heavens and the other plunged into the earth, of which no one, whether man or god, could ever learn how high it rose — higher than all heavens — or to what depth it descended — deeper than the very center of the earth....

•

It was surely fitting that a Christian also should come and worship in these high places, that he should come there to "fulfill" all signs, myths, and images, and to enable the vast sacrament of the cosmos to pass from the sign to its reality in Christ, in the Eucharist.

Beyond all question it is right and proper for the Christian, more than for any other, to come and meditate here on earth's ascent towards heaven through her snow-clad peaks, and on the descent from heaven to earth of the life-giving waters in the form of dark rain-clouds — and so of the meeting of both in the mystery of those high peaks, which seize and hold on their flanks the water of heaven and then pour it out in blessing on the earth.

Christ towers over all, the Everest of God's self-manifestation. He is the Source from which is poured out in torrents the grace and love of God. At Golgotha, from his side, pierced by the soldier's spear, sprang the church, and with it also the water and the blood, signs of the washing of rebirth and the life-giving chalice.

It was necessary that the Christ should tread the path up the Mountain which he himself is. It was necessary that in the person of his own he should climb up to *Himself,* in that pilgrimage which will only be completed on the Last Day at the final Consummation; for, according to St. Paul, the fullness of Christ will only be achieved when at last all are in him, and he himself is henceforth and forever all in all.

The time of the church is in truth nothing else than the completion of this ascent to the mystery of the Spirit. Indeed the church's continuance in the world and the Christian's pilgrim age are set in this time — the time of the ascent to Jerusalem, of the ascent to Calvary, of the return to the Source.

The Source is the Heart of Christ, the bosom of the Father.

— *Mountain,* 19–22

# 2

# *Advaita*

ॐ

*In January 1959, when Abhishiktananda had been in India for only a little over a year, he and Father Monchanin went to see the famous Indian sage Ramana Maharshi. This meeting was to bring about his real initiation into Indian spirituality.*

*Ramana was seventy at the time and very frail, so disciples were allowed into his presence only at certain times. At first Abhishiktananda was deeply disappointed, but late in the afternoon they returned to the* pandal, *the large open shelter where Ramana gave* darshan, *the word used for a "blessed seeing" when a devotee visits a holy man. Bhagavan, meaning "Lord," was the name by which Ramana was often known.*

## RAMANA MAHARSHI:
## "THE UNIQUE SAGE OF THE ETERNAL INDIA"

In the afternoon we returned to the *pandal*. About four or five o'clock the brahmins in the ashram came and sat around the couch on which Bhagavan was enthroned and began to chant the Vedas — a custom that is still faithfully observed to this day.

This was the first time that I was hearing that entrancing psalmody, with its strong rhythm and its simple melody within a range of only three or four notes. It carries one far back in time to the forest-hermitages of the ancient *rishis;* at evening, when the sun disappeared behind the horizon and the sacrificial flame rose up from their altars, they used to sing these very same verses and taught them to their disciples as a sacred trust for future generations of believers who would take their place in an endless succession on the soil of Bharat.

How far I felt myself from that everyday world in which I had been involved only a few hours before, from the crowds thronging the trains and railway-stations through which I had struggled to make my way during the previous night; how far equally from the glitter and false display which disfigured this *pandal,* how far even from this man — at least, in what he appeared outwardly to be — who provided the reason for the performance of this liturgy. These Vedic hymns, even when their outward meaning escapes one, have a uniquely penetrating power, at least for anyone who allows himself to be inwardly open to their spellbinding influence. We could say that, as they issue from the archetypal sources of being, so they irresistibly draw those who chant them, and equally those who hear them, into the same most secret sources of being. The mind thus finds itself carried off as if to an unknown world, a world in which however it has a marvelous sense of belonging, a world which is revealed in its very source, and yet which seems to disappear as soon as one attempts to define it in rational terms or to grasp it in concepts. I quickly gave up trying to understand it, and simply allowed myself to be held and carried along.... Even more strongly than the banks of the Kavery, for all their grandeur, Arunachala was beginning to claim me for itself.

At six o'clock the women left the ashram — this was a strict rule — and the screens were removed. Some people approached the Maharshi and began to put questions to him. His replies and the ensuing conversation were in Tamil, and this, added to the distance, made it unfortunately impossible for me to follow it.

Next morning I awoke with a fever. Nevertheless I went along to the *darshan* and at the beginning enjoyed once more the chanting of the Vedas. I allowed myself to be carried away by their spell; and I tried more than I had on the previous evening to penetrate behind the eyes of the Sage who was there before me, to find out his secret....

After the midday meal Purusha[1] took me to meet Miss Ethel, whom he had met on a previous visit. She asked for my impressions, and as I did not wish to conceal the truth, I told her of my disappointment. "You have come here with far too much 'baggage,'" she said. "You want to know, you want to understand. You are insisting that what is intended for you should necessarily come to you by the path which you have determined. Make yourself empty; simply be receptive: make your meditation one of pure expectation."

Purusha went off to take tea with another European family. I excused myself on the grounds of my cold, and went back to the *darshan,* muffled up to the eyes.

Did I really try to make myself empty on the lines suggested by Ethel? Or rather, did the fever which made me shiver get the better of all my efforts to meditate and reason? When the Vedas began again, their spell carried me off much further from things and from myself than had been the case on the previous evening. The fever, my sleepiness, a condition that was half dreaming, seemed to release in me zones of para-consciousness in which all that I saw or heard aroused overwhelmingly powerful echoes. Even before my mind was able to recognize the fact, and still less express it, the invisible halo of this Sage had been perceived by something in me deeper than any words. Unknown harmonies awoke in my heart. A melody made itself felt,

---

1. Abhishiktananda's nickname for Father Monchanin.

and especially an all-embracing ground bass.... In the Sage of Arunachala of our own time I discerned the unique Sage of the eternal India, the unbroken succession of her sages, her ascetics, her seers; it was as if the very soul of India penetrated to the very depths of my own soul and held mysterious communion with it. It was a call which pierced through everything, tore it apart, and opened a mighty abyss.   —*Secret,* 7–9

## RAMANA MAHARSHI'S WAY

The way that the Maharshi recommended is essentially positive. It consists in trying to find out at every instant, in every act, who in truth it is that lives, thinks, and acts, and in being attentive to the see-er in the act of seeing, to the hearer in the act of hearing, and so forth. It is a matter of constantly, relentlessly pursuing this consciousness of oneself which hides behind the phenomena and the events of the psychic life, of discovering it, seizing it in its original purity before anything else has covered it over or adulterated it. Thus seized it has to be held in the fine point of the spirit to prevent it from escaping again. This means in fact trying to reach one's self, one's identity, beyond and beneath the level of manifestation. Sri Ramana was perfectly sure that this investigation could not fail to bear fruit, provided it was pursued unflaggingly. The phenomenal self, the surface-I, if pursued to its last stronghold, will in the end disappear as if by magic, like a thief surprised in the act who runs for dear life. The essential *I* will then shine in solitary glory in the consciousness which has been stilled, and will fill it entirely.

> A ghost without a body, such is the I:
> in order to exist it borrows one;
> there it stays, feeds and grows.

> That body gone, it leaps on a new one.
> Search for it; already it has run away!
>
> Down to the place whence springs the I,
> plunge within thyself,
> like the diver searching for the pearl,
> his mouth closed and breath held.
>
> (adapted from *Ulladu Narpadu*, 25, 28)

If however anyone believed himself called to follow the more complicated paths of yoga, the Maharshi did not stand in his way. He never thrust his views upon anyone. When a man is not yet ready for it, why force him to take a path beyond his capacity? Why try to anticipate the hour? The Indian philosophy of *karma* teaches us to await the hour in patience and not to be discouraged on account of the slowness of man's personal growth. The goal will eventually be reached by each one at the moment appointed by destiny. For himself however Sri Ramana went directly to the essentials of yoga and invited those who entrusted themselves to him to do likewise, while he left to their illusions those who merely sought his approval for decisions which they had already taken.

There was just one breathing exercise which he did indeed recommend, but even that was only for those who had special difficulty in stifling their bodies and minds. This was to fix the attention on the act of breathing and consciously to follow the process of inhaling and exhaling — just as in the valuable practice of Japanese *za-zen*. Such attention and concentration of itself establishes a rhythm and automatically slows down the rate of breathing. The movement of the mind soon adjusts itself correspondingly, becomes more regular, slows down in its turn, and makes room for the inner silence.

— *Saccidananda*, 34–35

## RAMANA MAHARSHI — THE QUEST OF THE SELF

The "quest of the self" recommended by Sri Ramana Maharshi in its own way amounts to the same thing as that call to death which resounds throughout the Gospel, whose acceptance is paradoxically the very means of overcoming death by undergoing it. It also very closely resembles the *todo-nada* of St. John of the Cross. It may well be that the Vedantic paradoxes will help the Christian to gain a better understanding of the absolute claim upon him involved in his baptism into Christ's death and of the ever greater demands made by the Spirit within him.
— *Saccidananda*, 65

*So Abhishiktananda discovered* advaita, *which was to enrich his life immeasurably, but also to be the source of much pain and tension as he feared it would be impossible to reconcile with his deep-rooted Christianity.*

*The word* advaita *comes from the Sanskrit* a- *and* dvaita, *literally, "not two" — non-duality.*

## *ADVAITA* — A DEFINITION

*Advaita* is not so much a challenge to Christian faith as a relentless reminder that God — and therefore also the acts of God — can never be wholly contained in our concepts. It is a healthy and permanently necessary reminder of the importance of the "way of negation." It condemns, and at the same time frees us from, the idolatry of the intellect, in which our laziness and pride perpetually threaten to engulf us. It rejects the self-satisfied, characteristically bourgeois, reliance on institutions and rites which, however indispensable and sacramentally effective they may be, nevertheless are only signs. It delivers us from our very human tendency to transform the ineffable mystery of the Trinity into a kind of refined tritheism,[2] or at the other extreme, into simple modalism, despite the theoretical orthodoxy of our credal statements. It also frees us from the temptation somehow to "add up" God and ourselves, his creatures, on the grounds that we are not God — thus falling into a dualism no less contrary to the faith than monism.

All this constitutes a direct and inexorable attack on our congenital self-centeredness. Of ourselves we quite naturally judge everything from our own angle. We project God in front of us, and imagine him after our own image. Even the revelation that he has given us of his mystery has to pass through this mental bottleneck. Everything is subordinated to the fundamental assertion of this self of mine — a self that is moreover perilously restricted to the merely bodily and mental levels. If *advaita* appears to us as a threat, it is precisely because it will allow nothing to remain of that superficial bodily, or at best merely mental, ego which belongs to the level of concepts. It will never allow us to rest content with anything less than the "I" which God utters within himself, in the mysterious procession of the Word and the Spirit. The challenge of *advaita* is addressed, not to Christianity, but to the laziness and pride of Christians. It condemns their reluctance to accept once and for all these words of Jesus: "Whoever seeks to gain his life will lose it, but whoever loses his life will preserve it" (Luke 17:33). He has told us the inexorable law that governs the entry into life: "In order to be fruitful, a seed must fall into the ground and die" (cf. John 12:24).

There is no real contradiction between *advaita* and Christianity, but only between the false substitutes which usurp their

---

2. Tritheism, modalism — two opposite attempts (both unacceptable) to give a rational account of the Trinity; the former stressing the distinction of the Persons in such a way as to end in the affirmation of three Gods; the latter preserving the unity of God by reducing the Persons to mere "modes" or aspects of the One.

place, the premature and inadequate syntheses put forward on both sides by those who imagine that experience can be confined within their definitions.

Only the man who is ready to go to the end in the experience both of the Christian faith and of *advaita* will find the solution to the apparent antinomy. It is to be found in a higher light, which human reason alone will never to be able fully to account for. Even when enlightened by faith and guided by scripture and tradition, has man's reason ever been able to find an adequate expression of the mystery of grace, of God's concurrence in his own free action? The theologians who have attempted to do so have invariably got into difficulty by going to one or the other extreme, while mutually denouncing each other as heretics. In fact both sides have fallen victim to the same dualistic presupposition which assumes that God and man can be added together. But *advaita* means precisely this: neither God alone, nor the creature alone, nor God plus the creature, but an indefinable non-duality which transcends at once all separation and all confusion. — *Meeting Point,* 96–98

## THE CHALLENGE CHRISTIANITY AND *ADVAITA* PRESENT TO EACH OTHER

For the man who has direct experience of the Real nothing else remains except the naked uncompounded light of Being itself. One day someone asked Sri Ramana Maharshi why Christ taught his disciples to give God the name of Father. He answered, "Why should one not give God a name, so long as God remains for him 'another'?" Once a man has realized the truth, what room is left for anything like an *I* or a *Thou* or a *He?* Who is left even to whisper: "O my God, Thou alone art; I am nothing!"? In the blinding light of this experience there is no conceivable place for any kind of differentiation; there is nothing but *a-dvaita,* "not-two."

The Christian also is no doubt aware that God is in him and not merely that he comes to him (John 14:23; Rev. 3:20), and that the very center of his soul is God's dwelling place. He likewise knows that God is in all things; and in order to meet God he seeks to plunge deep within himself and within all things, in pursuit of his own and their final secret. The more he does this, the more he discovers the truth of God's presence, ever more luminous, more elemental. He then searches in the depths of his heart for a place where he might as it were stand and contemplate this Presence, the inner sanctum where his own incommunicable individuality issues from Being itself and springs into existence. He looks for that inner source from which his life and personal existence stream forth to be manifested on the outward plane of body and intellect. He seeks for that fine point of his consciousness, that "apex" of the soul, where more truly than anywhere else he might be himself in the presence of God, face to face with his Father, where he might be an *I* saying *Thou* to his God. Even if he must be consumed in the divine embrace for which the Spirit in him yearns (Song of Solomon 1:2), he wants at least to perceive himself at the moment of casting himself into this fire, and to be able to say to God, "I give myself to you."

Alas, when he tries to take his stand in the ultimate recesses of his self he finds that God is already there! He seeks vainly to recover his footing, so that he can withdraw into himself and try to save at least something of his own separate personal existence: like Moses and Elijah, he wants to hide in some cleft of the rock from which he may contemplate God. However, even the remotest and most inaccessible "caverns" of his heart turn out to be occupied already, and the darkness in which he had hoped to save his personal existence from annihilation in Being is already ablaze with the glory of God. He still struggles desperately to utter an *I*, a *Thou;* but now no sound makes itself heard, for *where* indeed could it come from? And even if by some means this *I* were to be pronounced, it would immediately be submerged in the one I AM that fills eternity, ... the thunder of Sinai, the immensity of waters mentioned in the Psalms. Like a shipwrecked sailor floundering in the high seas, tossed from wave to wave, he vainly struggles against the current that masters him and sweeps him away. All is up with him; soon there will no longer be any *I* to be conscious of any experience whatever, still less to be aware that all possible experiences are now finished. No one remains to say "I have reached the plane of the Absolute" — still less to say: "I have passed beyond, lost myself." Nothing is left, apart from that consciousness itself, pure and unalloyed: This *(tat)* ... that *(sat)* ... *OM* — "*OM tat sat,*" as the Gita says (17:23). For man cannot see God and live (Deut. 5:26). — *Saccidananda,* 63–65

## CHRISTIAN AND VEDANTIC ASCESIS

The *I* which is attacked initially by Christian ascesis is that superficial level of man's personality for which satisfaction is normally sought in the pursuit of success or the gratification of the senses. A slightly more refined ascesis includes the level of thought at which those who have given up their taste for outward things seek satisfaction by asserting themselves in more subtle and perhaps dangerous ways. However, when compared with the goal of Vedantic ascesis, all this seems a matter of externals only. Such an offering can hardly be described as a true sacrifice of the self; in it there is no sign of the holocaust in which nothing remains of the victim but ashes.

The target of Vedantic ascesis is something much deeper; it is nothing less than the actual *self* which is challenged in the very place of its origin, at the very moment of its awakening, before it has even begun to find expression. In the West there are not a few theologians who would maintain that this is too high a calling for the average Christian; but in India a *sadhana* which does not aim, at least ultimately, at this goal is not held to be worthy of the name. Vedantic ascesis seeks to strip man of his ego, his self, in a most radical fashion which no image or concept can adequately describe. Paradoxically one might perhaps say that it seeks to plunge the soul into that nothingness from which creation itself has come. It seeks relentlessly to experience the nothingness of all created being. As the Lord said to St. Catherine of Siena, "The creature *is not*;" only God *is*, and there is no one else beside him, before him or after him, who could say of him that "He is," or "He alone is." There is no loophole by which the mind can escape. And man can only be re-created in the very place in which he was created; his baptismal death plunges him into the very same nothingness out of which he was created, in order to raise him up again. Baptism necessarily involves this experience of death and nothingness. One cannot be a Christian at a lesser price.

—*Saccidananda*, 65–66

*Two questions constantly put by Ramana Maharshi were "Who am I?" and "What is the Self?" More and more Abhishiktananda became concerned with awareness, awakening, learning simply to "be."*

## SIMPLY BECOMING AWARE

It is the worst possible illusion to imagine that we have to struggle to find liberation or *mukti*, or to experience the self, which is the same thing. In truth, what is this world? or what is the other world? What does it mean to attain self-realization? or not to

# Advaita

have attained to it? To strive consciously and deliberately to arrive at this "realization of the self" is paradoxically the greatest obstacle in the way of reaching it; for it involves the assumption that man's natural state...is something that man does not yet possess — as if a man could *be* without being himself! Is a man really less of a man when sunk in deep slumber?

That *you are* my friend, you know well. Your experience every moment reminds you of it. Simply find out *who* you are, find out what it is in you that does not depend on the changing circumstances of your bodily or mental existence, that kernel of your consciousness which, in the last analysis, cannot be identified with any of the external circumstances in which you find yourself. Do not waste time in negating the passing identities of which you are momentarily conscious, for that will only detain and hinder you. Pass beyond; discover in yourself that which is free and independent of all around or within you that changes or passes away. In every deed, every act of will, every thought, ask yourself the essential question: "*Who* is thinking, willing, acting? Who am *I*, the actor behind the action, the thinker behind the thought, the one who wills behind the act of willing?" To this question your mind, becoming increasingly bewildered, will less and less know what to answer. Your thought will be hopelessly bound to the shifting world of phenomena, the world of all that ceaselessly appears and disappears when perceived by sense or mind. In all this there is nowhere any stable point to which you can succeed in fastening your fundamental intuition that you *are:* yet you *are*, with no possibility of saying where you are, what you are, who you are....

...This method leaves no place for subconscious transference or for the inflation of the ego. It is through and through a method of relaxation, of detachment, of flight towards what is inward and authentic. It allows no attention to oneself. At one and the same time it is liberating and supremely demanding. As an ascesis (discipline) which is more radical than any other, it excludes even the slightest effort of a man's will towards a self-chosen goal. It cuts at the very root of any self-satisfaction and so achieves the most radical purification. At the heart of every thought it inserts like a red-hot iron the *neti-neti* of the Upanishads, the "not that, nor yet that," which utterly rules out the possibility of halting on the quest. Once again this *neti-neti* is certainly not an idea in which the mind might seek at least some rest and relief. At the heart of thought itself *neti-neti* is already essential awareness, deep experience, hidden, yet burning and devouring....

The mind then realizes more and more its inability to say: "I am this or that; I am this person or that person." For in the very moment at which the thought appears that I am this or that, this person or that person, then this manifestation with which I have automatically tried to identify myself in the flow of consciousness has fled away from me — but *I* continue. Sensory and psychic experience flow on in a steady stream which nothing can stop, being part of that constant succession of change which is the nature of the cosmos. While this flow continues endlessly, I myself abide, *I am,* in an unchanging present. All things pass, change; but as for me, I *am*. What am I? Who am I? There is no answer except the pure awareness that *I am,* transcending all thought.

"I am," and there is no need for me to strive in order to find this "I am." I am not an "I" searching for itself. The Maharshi pointed this out very astutely when certain disciples sought by means of thought and reasoning to realize "who they were," and thus engaged themselves in an endless mental pursuit of this elusive self. The search is endless because the self which is *thought* poses the problem of the self which *thinks,* and so on *ad infinitum.* All that a man has to do is simply to allow himself to be grasped by this light which springs up from within, but itself cannot be grasped. Who can ever savor the taste of absolutely pure water? So also with pure air, who will ever see it or smell it?

Awake, O man, and realize simply that you *are*. You are neither the butterfly dreaming that it is the king nor the king dreaming that he is the butterfly, as in the Chinese proverb. *You are yourself.* Indian folklore preserves the tale of the lion cub whose parents had been killed by hunters and which was reared along with a flock of sheep. He learned to bleat and to eat grass, and grew up without suspecting that he himself was not a lamb. One day a lion fell upon the flock. Seeing the lion cub he asked him what he was doing among the sheep and why he was not ashamed of bleating and eating grass. "But am I not a lamb?" replied the astonished cub. Then the lion took him to a pool of water and told him to look at their two faces reflected in it and to compare them. "Are you not the same as I am? Is it not your nature to drink blood and to roar? Come, roar like I do...." The cub roared, and as he roared he recognized himself....

So it is with the soul which awakes to the Self.

—*Saccidananda*, 38–40

## MAN IS TRULY HIMSELF

Man is truly *himself* in fact at a deeper level than that on which he philosophizes. Of course he will never despise that level of being at which he thinks and at which, through the medium body, he enters into communion with his fellowmen and with the universe. So too he will never become indifferent to that level of himself through which he shares in the vast process of evolution — cosmic, biological, and human — which extends from the emergence of the primordial atom to the final handing over of all things by Christ into his Father's hands. But all this he lives from within that inner sanctuary where he abides in the transparent purity of his consciousness of being. He lives it from the very center of his being, from that very source in which he comes into being as the image of God. Human evolution, alike in the individual and in society, proceeds from the circumference to the center, starting with those coarse and superficial levels of being in which of necessity man's life had to remain for so long — and in which lamentably too many still choose to remain at their peril — and reaching at last that point where the Self is revealed in the self. — *Saccidananda,* 69

## THERE IS ONLY BEING

My Hindu and advaitin submersion plunges me more and more into Unity. Being is inexpressible. In the within there is only Being. And the distinctions whether in God in the full possession of Being, or among the creatures in the participation of Being, have nothing to do with Being. There is no BEING and BEING. Coming back into the within, there is nothing other than Being and only he who possesses Being quite fully, he only can truly say I. Saturn and Jupiter and Venus are visible because they are far from the sun. Mercury is barely. And if there is some other planet closer to the center, who will be able to make it out? He who penetrates to the Center, the within, to the essential I, to the essential HIMSELF, how will he discern from then on what he used to call I, me, him? "Used to..." but these words themselves sound wrong. The within has nothing more to do with, nothing in common with time. Everything which has direction, notion of past, future, is of the without, the unreal....

So what is this distinction which has nothing to do with Being? — JL, April 20, 1953, *Lettres,* 78

## ETERNITY

Eternity is in the passing moment; but to want to remain in the moment that has passed or to go ahead to the moment that is coming is to abandon eternity for time. Eternity is not in the time that lasts but in the indivisible moment.

Offer to God the eternal offering of the eternal moment, just as it is in me, in my body, and in my consciousness, in the creation around me, in the entire creation, in the birds that sing, in the flowers that open and close, and the water that flows down the hillside, and the wind that plays in the trees and the clouds that float across the sky, the sun that gives light and warmth, and the people who work and struggle, who suffer and rejoice, who love and give themselves, those whom this moment causes to live as one with me, and all people of all times....

Make the offering of this moment and receive the gift of this moment. The gift of this moment to me is the reality no other than the gift to the Son of the eternity springing up from the heart of the Father.

> To accept it is to offer it.
> To know it is to rejoice with the Bliss of the Spirit.
> To accept it: faith;
> To know it, rejoice in it, is to love with the Spirit's love.
> It is to be fulfilled, to let oneself be fulfilled in the
>     inbreathing of the Spirit,
> and to be fulfilled in the Spirit is to fulfill God,
> who without fulfillment through us at this moment in the
>     Spirit
> could not be fulfilled in himself in eternity, in his Spirit.
>     For my moment is God's eternity.

—June 8, 1952, *Diary*, 44

## ETERNITY IN THE PRESENT MOMENT

Shantivanam, November 16, 1961

Everything is straightforward, once one has grasped that quite simply God is Father and that only in him one *is*. Everything is love and everything is divine begetting, and everything is response to this divine begetting in love. Everything is light, and in the bright light of the Trinity there are no shadows. We only have to gaze. Men struggle and the Lord uses them to bring his Christ to birth. And he shows clearly that after all he does not have any need for us. He plays tricks with us, or else sets us in enforced leisure, or again quite simply he summons us to Paradise (like Father X), even though we think that we still have some work to do for him. Time counts for so little. The one important thing is to lay hold of eternity at this present moment, to center oneself in the very process of the begetting of the Son of God, proceeding forth in the eternal present from the Father's bosom, and yet eternally established in him. And I believe that it is truly there that we finally do our work. It is at the "heart" of man, of the Christ, of the Father, in the *guha,* the cave of the heart, that the church is born and grows, that faith spreads and grace is imparted. It is in and through these mystical springs that the Sacrament obtains its fullest efficacy. But who is ready to work solely within the divine begetting? At least to *start* his work there, what follows being only effective to the extent that it manifests, expresses, and radiates this inner mystery?   —FT, *LS&T,* 133

## GOAL OF THE UNIVERSE

The goal of the universe is the consciousness of being, the final unveiling of the intuition that constitutes the human being. There were sages, there were seers, there were prophets, and each of them grasped something of the mystery within, the mystery within every being. And their intuitions are stars, beacons for their brothers. From the shore they send a signal, and on the rock they have lighted a flame. And this flame is a call.

— October 22, 1966, *Diary*, 286

*Consciousness of simply "being" more and more permeated Abhishiktananda's life and writings. These short extracts from his* Spiritual Diary *and from his letters show this deep engagement.*

## BEING

My work is to be. The really important times in my life: those when I simply am, established within. To these times everything is ordered, those times are not ordered to the times when I am working. — July 5, 1973, *Diary*, 384

"There is only one thing that is real, the present moment in which I am face-to face with God.... We are like rich people with any amount of money who waste time marveling at their small change. I have only one sermon: "Realize what you are at this very moment; contemplate your being at the heart of the Trinity, where you have been placed by your baptism, your communion; and be faithful to yourselves, to what you are. Become what you are!" — MT, August 21, 1960, *LS&T*, 129

Westerners are always anxious to be *doing!* but we come to India, and there we learn simply *to be;* and be-ing is the most intense form of action. No external movement in the physical world is so intense as the movement at the heart of the atom, through which indeed it exists. So it is with us.

— MT, March 19, 1959, *Life*, 130

The Ganga is there, and I am learning simply to gaze at it. This simple act of looking, just gazing, with no further thought either of the one who is looking, or of the look itself, or of what is looked at — is so difficult for our Western mentality.
— TJ, April 18, 1970, *LS&T,* 146

I really believe that the revelation of the *AHAM* is perhaps the central point of the Upanishads. And that is what gives access to everything; the "knowing" which reveals all the "knowings." God is not known, Jesus is not known, nothing is known, outside this terribly "solid" *AHAM* that I am.
— MC, October 20–21, 1973, *Life,* 356

And then the Lord takes you seriously, removes every fine thought and leaves you there, capable of nothing more than simply being there! And that is what is most real.
— FT, November 30, 1973, *Life,* 361

A being lost in my source, a being lost in my fulfillment. And in this very loss, I am.... — December 24, 1971, *Diary,* 336

God is only another name of being, of being when it is looked in the face.... But can God look himself in the face? God does not look at himself; if he could look at himself, how would he still be God? — July 2, 1954, *Diary,* 95

*3*

# East-West

ॐ

*Abhishiktananda was a devout Roman Catholic, whose belief in Christ nourished and sustained him all his life, yet now he found himself irresistibly drawn to Hindu* advaita. *This caused him the most terrible pain and anguish: How could he follow both paths? He summed up his dilemma in a few words in his* Spiritual Diary, *after only a few years in India: "For now I have tasted too much of* advaita *to be able to recover the "Gregorian" peace of a Christian monk. Long ago I tasted too much of the "Gregorian" peace not to be anguished in the midst of my* advaita."[1]

*While the anguish this tension caused him brought him years of suffering, it also concerned him intellectually, as he strove to reconcile the two.*

## *ADVAITA* AND THE RELIGIONS

Christians in India are confronted with a spiritual and religious experience which, no less than theirs, claims to be ultimate. In the name of that experience Hindu sages and mystics vie with each other in asserting the essentially relative status of whatever

---

1. September 27, 1953, *Diary,* 74.

is accessible to human sense or reason. Under this judgment they include without exception, not only the truths that men can discover through the intellects but also those that they claim to have received directly from God through divine revelation. Beliefs, rites and religious institutions of every kind fall under that general devaluation.

The Hindu *jnani* [sage] does not of course deny all value to Christian faith and institutions. He considers them to be useful and indeed beneficial for people of a particular cultural background, so long as their spiritual experience is still confined to the sphere of time and multiplicity. This indeed holds true not merely for Christianity but for all religions, not least for Hinduism itself. So long as a man differentiates between the *I*, the world, and God, for him dogmas and rites are not merely legitimate but necessary. No one has any right to evade the obligations of his own *dharma,* so long as he has not yet reached the final experience. It is not enough that he should have read in the scriptures or heard from his guru that ultimate truth is *advaita*, or non-duality. The liberty that is inherent in the state of deliverance is won by experience alone. No purely intellectual conviction obtains it, for every act of the intellect inevitably remains on the dualistic level of ordinary experience.

From a Vedantic point of view neither Hindu scriptures and worship nor Christian dogmas and sacraments have an ultimate value. They are all like the raft of which the Buddha often spoke. One makes use of it to cross a river, and in an emergency if none is available, one might even construct a raft oneself; but no one would dream of taking it with him, once he has reached the other bank. Again, they are like the lighted taper, spoken of in the Upanishads: one makes use of it to light the lamp, but it is put aside without further thought, once the lamp is lit. Man is capable of true consciousness of the Self. He is not made to remain forever on the rudimentary level of consciousness to which sense perception, directed as it must be towards what is external, draws him and at which it seeks to hold him. The infant, to be sure, at first has need of milk, but milk is not going to be his food forever. He needs at first his mother's breast, but life at his mother's breast is not man's final state. No more can the butterfly remain at the stage of the chrysalis. The same applies to the successive stages through which man passes in his mental and spiritual development, from the practical thinking of primitive man to the reflective thought of the philosopher, and finally the unalloyed self-consciousness of the seer.

— *Saccidananda,* 43

## THE ADVAITIC DILEMMA

If Christianity should prove to be incapable of assimilating Hindu spiritual experience from within, Christians would thereby at once lose the right to claim that it is the universal way of salvation. Christianity could not be "another" peak of spiritual experience alongside that of Vedanta, nor could its way of salvation be "another" parallel way. In their claim to be ultimate, Christianity and *advaita* are mutually exclusive. And yet, in its own sphere, the truth of *advaita* is unassailable. If Christianity is unable to integrate it in the light of a higher truth, the inference must follow that *advaita* includes and surpasses the truth of Christianity and that it operates on a higher level than that of Christianity. There is no escape from this dilemma.

This of course is not to say that Vedantic philosophy would not have to be reformulated if it is to express the Christian experience. The Christian way in its inmost essence is a passing through death and resurrection, and this applies as much to what it takes in from outside as to its own development. Nothing that comes into contact with the Incarnation can escape this law. Christianity takes hold of what is natural, rids it of everything in it that is relative and subject to decay, and raises it to a higher level, that of grace. At this level nature finds itself again, entirely renewed from within and seemingly transformed in its innermost being; yet it is not changed into something different, but as it were into a still deeper reality and truth of its own being (cf. 1 Cor. 15.35ff.). Thus it was with the human nature which was assumed by the Lord. Thus also it is with the human personality of each one who responds to the Spirit and reaches the state of being a son of God. Thus too it is with human society and culture as it passes into the church, or the *pleroma* of Christ. —*Saccidananda,* 49

## WHY NAME THE MYSTERY?

Why want at all costs to name the mystery that is within me? Under the name of Jesus, I entered marvelously into it, and this heart of Jesus, my heart, appeared to me as the Father's bosom. Under the name of Arunachala, I next entered into it and then the sight was so great that it dazzled me; and all the names, all the forms that until then I had distinguished within it under the guidance of my previous masters vanished in this full sunlight. But when the sun has appeared, have the stars left their place in the firmament? And has the moon stopped in its orbit?

Wanting to give it a name, in that lies all the trouble. Do not name it, gaze, be dazzled, "be"; do not give a name to it, but be this mystery. And I am it....

—November 15, 1956, *Diary,* 163, quoted in SETU (Bulletin of the Abhishiktananda Society), no. 24

## THE WEST'S INTEREST IN THE EAST

The increasing interest that the West is showing in the East is certainly one of the most hopeful signs in the crisis sweeping the world at this time. Western man has indeed much to learn of this spiritual and cultural world of the East which has evolved in such a very different way from his own. Perhaps it is only there that he will discover the inferiority which he so patently lacks and will recover the identity which he has lost, but this time it will be an identity which will reveal to him the very depth of his own being.

This does not, of course, mean that just any contact with the East will enable the Westerner to have access to her true riches; it would be even more untrue to imagine that such a contact would act like a panacea to cure all the evils from which society is suffering today. Besides, the East and the West are complementary; each has as much to receive from the other and in totally different spheres. But this exchange will be completely beneficial only if it takes place on the proper level, failing which the East can never be discovered in her real depth. On other levels, when the exchange is not complementary, there is a risk of dangerous traumatic experiences being provoked in one way or another. One need only think of the ravages that are sometimes caused by the brutal introduction of techniques into a social milieu which is unprepared no matter how much prestige they may bring. No exchange is truly profitable unless it takes place as communion in the deepest depths of people's beings. It is only in this depth, peculiar to each one and yet where all may mysteriously communicate, that men coming from diverse cultures and traditions are capable of meeting and of recognizing one another, of each discovering his identity in a most personal way and, at the same time, of accepting the most marvelous pluralism of individuals and cultures. Thanks to this, each then finds in the other his own blossoming and spiritual advancement.

The sad thing is that when the West approaches the East to ask her secret, she too often goes about it in the wrong way. Even today, though it is less common than previously, the West will accost the East with that pride and sense of racial and cultural superiority which marked the colonial epoch. There can obviously then be neither communion nor true exchange. Even when the West enrolls herself in the school of the East in apparent humility and sincerity, she does so too often in an attitude of false passivity which makes her at least hope for, if not demand, an immediate reply to her problems and one, furthermore, which must fit into her own categories. It is precisely this quest, wrongly understood and wrongly taken in hand, that at the present time is launching so many young and not so young people "on the road to Katmandu," in search of the sages and gurus of Rishikesh, Benares, and other places. Alas, it is a search that is seldom successful and too often ends only in disappointment and frustration, with these unfortunate people harshly accusing India of not conforming to their own preconceived ideas.

The majority of these seekers in fact forget to begin by emptying their souls of all that is useless and extraneous, and by opening themselves to their true depths where alone it is possible to receive India's message. This message gushes forth on all sides in India; from the temples and holy places and, above all, from the holy men, who are by no means scarce, whatever may be said to the contrary; but one must know how to hear the message and how to meet these true spiritual masters. In truth there is passivity and passivity. There is one form of passivity which is all acceptance and receptivity, all "listening," like a radio set perfectly tuned and free from interference, ready to pick up the waves transmitted through space. There is another form of passivity, which is unfortunately the more common one, which refuses every attempt at assimilation and has not the least desire to clear the mind of prejudices and preoccupations: if one does not bother to open the shutters how can one expect even the midday sun to come into the room?

— *Guru and Disciple*, 5–7

## THE CHALLENGE PRESENTED TO CHRISTIANITY

The challenge presented to Christianity by *advaita* is indeed the challenge offered by man himself as he is destined to be when he reaches that high point of consciousness to which he is called and towards which his own nature draws him. And yet it is not so much a challenge as a summons. For the most significant stages in the history of the world are marked out by the successive steps in man's progress towards the Self, as he ceaselessly advances towards and attains to himself, and yet always desires to find himself more fully, more deeply still. It is a summons to a totally liberated consciousness of self such as is the goal of the psychic development of the individual and of the cultural and religious evolution of human societies. Unceasingly and painfully, like a woman in travail (to use St. Paul's metaphor in Rom. 8:22), this humanity-to-be cries out to Christ and to the church in whom Christ lives, that the Incarnation should be brought to bear upon the very core of human nature, its awareness of self, which is at once its source and fulfillment. In principle of course, this has been accomplished once and for all in the union of God and man in the person of Christ, and its realization is anticipated in the faith and sacraments of the church. But the Spirit and grace of God can never rest until this faith blossoms into the experience of wisdom and until the sacrament brings forth in the soul of the believer that spiritual fullness of which it is the sign and the vehicle. The *pleroma* of Christ will never be the fullness that it is intended to be, either in the individual believer or in the church at large, so long as that experience has not been integrated by Christianity.

It is reasonable to hope that when at last Christianity seriously sets out to lead man towards this inner awakening to himself, then the Christian faith will make a decisive impact on the world and the church will shine out in all its glory. It is indeed a great cause of stumbling that the leaven of the Gospel has been so slow to penetrate the mass of humanity. The law of love has been preached for two thousand years, and yet the world, even the Christian world, is still plagued by fratricidal struggles whose total incompatibility with the Gospel is felt by only a tiny minority of the faithful. It is two thousand years since Christ taught his disciples that only one thing was required of them, namely, to follow his example in serving others; and yet human society, including Christian society, is still based on selfishness, the profit motive, power, and the exploitation of the weak. All his life Paul fought to free the church from the Jewish legalism that hindered the Spirit from bearing fruit in the lives of Christians; but it was not long before the old spirit of Judaism reasserted its influence. As a result the church came to look very similar to any other human institution, while Christianity came to resemble the other competing religions in the world and all too often seemed to have lost its original awareness of mystery, as was very courageously admitted at the Second Vatican Council. —*Saccidananda*, 70–71

## A CALL TO THE CHURCH

Anyone who disdainfully rejects a priori the experience of the depths to which the Vedantic tradition bears witness only proves thereby the meanness of his spirit and the shallowness of his own spiritual experience; he is like the landlubber who decides that the ocean is a myth. Moreover it is useless merely to assert flatly that this experience is not compatible with the Gospel. The advaitic experience is the acme of man's spiritual experience in the cosmic religions. If Christianity should refuse to integrate it, then, as we have already said, that would amount to accepting the postulate that Christian faith is of a non-transcendental order. It would be to admit that it corresponds to a certain stage in the evolution of the human consciousness and therefore possesses spiritual value only for a given period of history and in a given area of culture.

—*Saccidananda,* 68

## THE TENSION BETWEEN CHRISTIANITY AND HINDU *ADVAITA*

*The extent to which Abhishiktananda was torn between Hinduism and Christianity is shown most poignantly in this passage, written to his old friend Canon Lemarié. It shows Abhishiktananda still in the grip of his old-fashioned Catholicism, yet attracted beyond resisting by Hindus and their religion, so much so that though he has only been in India a few years, he refers to the Hindus as "my people."*

*Advaita* is so overpowering — disappearance in the One! And so is Hindu worship, at least in its purest manifestation — the offering of flowers and milk to the bare stone — phallic-shaped, but nothing obscene in the idea — placed in the holy of holies, the cave, that small dark chamber deep in the heart of the temple, which one only reaches after passing through numerous courtyards and halls. When in certain (Shivaite) temples I am allowed to enter there, I cannot but feel close to them; their symbolic worship, adumbrations that are incomplete rather than false.... I am torn, rent in two, between Christ and my brothers; my brothers more even than my blood.... When I pray "through Christ," they cannot follow me. And I can no longer rejoice in our feasts as formerly, because my people are not with me. And I cannot unite myself to my people in their symbolic worship, because I am a priest of the true worship, and thus I fail to have communion with my people in what is the highest and most divine in them. The husband who cannot sit at the communion table next to his wife. And I endeavor to work back to Christ, taking as my starting point the thought and religious devotion of my people. (Suppose) the eternal Hindu *sannyasi* who one day on the way met Christ, but alas, Christ speaks and understands a Western language, is dressed in Western clothes! In India Jesus would have been dressed like me, of that I am sure. I like that series of Protestant pictures, in which Christ is wearing a simple *dhoti* around his waist and a *tundu* over his shoulder. The picture of the Transfiguration is really a Krishna transformed into Christ.... What is terrible is that my people have no need of Christ. They admire him, they love him, his picture is in many ashrams, but to consider him as the one and only way to God! Christ is "creature" and therefore steeped in *maya* as are all creatures! The mystery of Advent has no sense for the Hindu. I was thrown by this the other month. The greatest say: "Why search for salvation without: realize who you are: one whose very depth is one with God."

—JL, February 10, 1952, *Lettres* 37, quoted in *Life*, 59

*Many of his writings on the tension between Christianity and advaita are in his book* Saccidananda, *which was originally published in French, with the title* Sagesse hindoue mystique chrétienne. *Its publication brought encouraging responses from people who found it helped them to understand their own experiences. Thirty-five years later, more and more people are having these experiences, which is partly why Abhishiktananda is so relevant today. When it was first published in 1965, people found they could relate to Abhishiktananda's experience of the Self, which he describes in the first chapters. Abhishiktananda was touched by these responses.*

## RESPONSES TO *SACCIDANANDA*

My book *Sagesse* has brought me several moving testimonies from contemplatives (Christians), who for the first time in their life have recognized their own experience in the experience of the Self which I described in the first chapters. At noon today I received another shattering letter on this subject. Even John of the Cross, said the writer, had not been able to explain so clearly the interior stripping (nudity) and the passage from the "self" to the "Self" (words used spontaneously by this person, despite the shock given to his rational mind). How clearly it spells out the universal — and so, Christian, *katholikos* — value of the advaitin experience. What is needed above all is to invite Christians to make this experience their own. Otherwise the theological conclusions that we draw from this experience will continue to seem unthinkable or blasphemous. It is therefore only in a deepening of contemplative awareness in the church that there lies any hope of the ecumenical and "pan-ecumenical" passing beyond that we need. That can never happen at today's ordinary level of awareness. Until then there is only the loneliness of the prophet...and the impossibility of being at one's ease anywhere except with those few people who have an intuition of this "trans-cendent" level — like traveling faster than sound, or escaping from the earth's gravity, to use physical metaphors.... — RP, July 5, 1966, *Life,* 204

You cannot be torn apart in the depth of your soul, as we are by this double summons (from advaitin India on one side, and from Revelation on the other), and by this double opposition (from India and the church, in their ritualism, their formalism, and their intellectualism), without being lacerated even physically.... Yet another letter from Europe strengthens my conviction that the advaitin experience underlies all true mysticism, Christian included. All these letters in short say this:

"Your book has taught me nothing new, but for the first time in my life I have understood what was happening in my soul." That consoles one for many things, doesn't it? It is just one more proof that we are not heading in the wrong direction.
—RP, *July 15, 1966, Life,* 204–5

*Friends were always an important part of Abhishiktananda's life, and it must have been a great relief to him to find that there were many people to whom he was able to write about his personal agony.*

## TENSIONS

Easter is the great passing over to the pure reality of *advaita*. But how agonizing it is to be perched on the knife-edge between the opposite slopes of Hinduism and Christianity.
—JL, *April 4, 1954, Life,* 79–80

I should now leave it behind and find Christianity at the very heart of *advaita*. The intellect toils and turns and twists and is put out of joint. The heart smiles: How uselessly you give yourself trouble.... The truth is altogether more simple!
—JL, *July 24, 1954, Life,* 82

What contrasts! I do my best to be at ease everywhere, but there is an inevitable tension. But it is precisely this being torn apart between India and Europe, between Vedanta and Christianity which enables me to live the fundamental *experience* and to express its mystery to some extent.
—MT, *September 25, 1966, Life,* 207

I know something about this myself, living as I do half with the established church and half with those who possess nothing, half with Christians and half with Hindus — a very uncomfortable situation, believe me! It is here that I find your point about the "bridge" very illuminating. It is precisely the fact of being a bridge that makes this uncomfortable situation worthwhile. The world, at every level, needs such bridges. If, to be a Hindu with Hindus, I had become a complete *sannyasi,* I would have been unable to communicate either the Hindu message to Christians or the Christian message to Hindus.... However, the danger of this life as a "bridge" is that we run the risk of not belonging finally to either side; whereas, however harrowing it may be, our duty is precisely to belong wholly to both sides. This is only possible in the mystery of God.

—AMS, February 9, 1967 *Life,* 213

...but how can we reconcile the Patristic tradition, the Vedantic tradition, and the aspirations of the modern spirit?

—MT, October 2, 1968, *Life,* 231

I know what it is to be torn in pieces.

—AG, June 20, 1972, *LS&T,* 155

# 4

# Immersion in Hinduism

ॐ

*Abhishiktananda's great contribution to interfaith dialogue was immeasurably enhanced by the depth of his knowledge and understanding of Hinduism, which was generally considered to be exceptional in a European. He achieved this by immersing himself in it, embracing every aspect of its faith and culture. The man who had come to India with the intention of spreading the Christian message learned to be humble in the face of this great tradition, to be open and transparent. The following article, addressed to Westerners coming to India, was written with his great friend Murray Rogers.*

## PRAY TO BE SIMPLY TRANSPARENT

You belong perhaps to a famous order or monastery and maybe you think, not unnaturally, that what made your order or monastery so fruitful in the West is precisely what India needs today. There are many people here already who propose detailed methods both of mission and of doctrinal and spiritual formation, who anticipate even minutiae such as timetable, dress, and the way of recruiting of the group they want to found.

Humbly but firmly we tell you, please leave in the West all the glory of your religious community, of your monastery.

Leave behind the outward expression of the spirit which animates your order and come yourself alone, you as the Spirit has made you through your particular community. Please do not bring here either your prestige or your formulas; bring us your spirit — only your spirit at its very source. There is no need for new foundations of orders and monasteries; already, perhaps, we have too many of them. What we need are monks, souls who have opened themselves, in their very depth, to the life of the Spirit within, who have listened within to the voice of the Spirit calling to the Father, who have heard within the very silence of the Father. There is no need for transplanted trees; we need the seeds, the seeds which will be entrusted to the rich soil of India and which in time will bear a wonderful harvest, always provided the seed is good and the ground well chosen.

Come first among us without anybody knowing who you are, except for a few friends who will help you in the first steps of your pilgrimage. Pray to be simply transparent, open your eyes, open your ears, fill your lungs, let your whole self be stroked by the wind around you. Make yourself completely teachable and receptive; let nothing come between you and the Spirit. Let the Spirit capture in you, for you, the riches which he has prepared for you in India, in her scriptures, her traditions, her sages.

Many people feel greatly disappointed when they actually meet India; they have imagined India in their own way, like this...like that...but India is neither like this, nor like that, either on the material plane or on the spiritual. India is herself. Naturally enough, like every "person," India has her less attractive side, even repulsive, but for those who penetrate deeper India is a revelation of God. Indeed we believe that in our time India has a message from God for the world, and perhaps for Christians first, a message which calls irresistibly towards the depth within, this depth which is so largely ignored, or even put to one side by so many in the West, who think themselves wise even on the spiritual plane.

At this point may we tell you that as long as this depth has remained unplumbed by the witnesses of Christ in this land their words remain "a sounding gong" and "a clanging cymbal." Their message is not heard, their very witness remains empty. Therefore come first to listen to India. Make yourself a child in order to receive from her her own message for you, to listen in the depth of your heart, to overhear in the depth of your soul her own waiting for God. Then, and then only, will it be possible to know at which point of the tree it will be good to make a graft.

Make yourself small, and listen. Mix unknown with the crowd whose wisdom is often great under a rough exterior; mix with those who study and who so often reject old tradition and religion, and discover in the depth of their souls their burning thirst for God, a thirst which is part of the age-long religious thirst of India, and which Christianity in its so exclusively Western garb is unable to satisfy. Let the Spirit mold you little by little; let the grain die in the earth first, and then secretly germinate, first within the earth, later slowly to appear.

Of course this will not happen without pain. Nothing is born without pain since the Garden of Eden; the church sprang from the pierced heart of Christ on the Cross, and even now the church is being born in each soul, in each people, in each race — a birth which is death and resurrection together, a giving up of all the past and a receiving of it anew. The completion of this rebirth of India in Christ awaits our readiness for it to take place first in us — at any price God may ask — in our bodies, in our hearts, in our minds. We must return to the womb of the church, the womb of India — to the bosom of the Father. When the time comes, then with Christ we shall appear in glory too; but first let us remain, like John, in the desert till the time marked by God for his manifestation.

Resist firmly the temptation which will come to you from the church on your arrival, or even perhaps before you arrive, if you are not hidden enough. Many, especially Christian leaders, will want to make use of you immediately; they will ask you to teach at once in the church, to explain to Christians here your ways of worship, of prayer, of spiritual training — and indeed the church here has much to learn from you — but first you must learn from India. The success of your immediate work will simply jeopardize the lasting value which should come later from your presence in India, once you have imbibed the Indian spirit and understood her real religious needs. In the beginning you will only be able to speak and to act as Westerners, as foreigners, for even things, ideas, and methods which seem to you of universal value are held by you in a European manner. You will have to strip them from their European background and context before being able to make them truly profitable in the Indian "world."

Let us warn you also against another temptation, that is, to be anxious to develop a group in India, to try to be busy with recruiting followers, postulants, vocations as they say. Come here and think of the Lord alone; he himself will look after your concerns. As it has been said here for centuries, neither the rose nor the lotus flower need to advertise their blossoming; bees themselves will know the time and the way to come. Indeed who can be so daring as to think himself able to be a guru as long as the Lord has not indicated it clearly by sending disciples? Recruiting, practiced here too much already, smacks of human activism. God keep you free from it until his own time comes.

— A Letter from India, written with C. Murray Rogers, *One in Christ*, vol. 3, 1967, 196–98

*During 1952 and 1953 Abhishiktananda wrote a book that he called* Guhantara. *The title means "one who lives in a cave," symbolically in the depths of the heart. He was later to say of it:* "Guhantara *for me is the direct expression of my first intense 'dazzling.'* " *It is not hard to understand his intense disappointment when the book was rejected by the Censor, whose report was "totally damning, attacking the book on every conceivable ground, and finding 'heresies' on every page. It was so totally negative as to be ludicrous" (James Stuart,* Life, *83). To this day only extracts of it have been published; this is a slightly shortened version of one of them.*

## THE GRACE OF INDIA

The grace of India is a grace of interiority. Insofar as one lives the inner life oneself, one is capable of understanding India, and also of being accepted and understood by India. Conversely, insofar as one penetrates the secret of India, one discovers oneself in the within, one penetrates the unfathomable depth of oneself more and more deeply. No message from the West, even were it gathered up and sent by the Word of God, will ever succeed in awakening a deep echo in the soul of India, unless it is presented in the guise of the "within."

India can certainly live very much "without." Her worship is often clothed in very outward forms, sometimes even vulgar. And then one is surprised to see pure and profound souls taking part in such demonstrations. But precisely this life of the within, this worship of the without, are only ever the *lila*, the stake — the "divine play" of the Lord in and through his creation. India would never know how to take it totally seriously. Or rather if she were playing with conviction and the requisite seriousness, she would always know that this was happening in the sphere of time and space, and had no definitive value.

For the true Hindu, Hinduism would never think of itself without an opening at the summit, without that essential outlet to the transcendent Mystery in which he surpasses himself by reaching completion. And is that not the unique greatness of Hinduism, how much more characteristic really of its deep and actual spirit than the superstitions and degeneration into which it sometimes sinks, that sense of its own completion achieved only by surpassing itself, and does it not testify to the deep truth that is part of the essential intuition of the Prophets from which it springs?

Nothing "is" truly unless it is the Supreme, the *Brahman* who is beyond any name. "He is played out in the birth, duration, and destruction of all worlds," as Ramanuja chants, at the beginning of his Shri Bhashya. The devout person also plays a part in the "divine play" of his Lord. He gives himself up to it as one does to a dream — a dream vigil is understood. He takes part in it as would an actor in a theater play. He plays his role with all sincerity, being joyful, being sad, without the background ever being affected, however, the Real, which remains an impassive witness of the action of the scene, unshakeable and fixed in the Absolute. India knows that when prostrating herself before an idol, that idol is just stone or metal, but also that this is a necessary relay to penetrate to the beyond. When she reads her Puranas — the myths handed down by tradition — she is not troubled by the stories she reads about the gods. She knows that in fact all of it is symbolic. Brahma, Vishnu, and Shiva themselves, not to mention the other divine forms, exist only in the world of *maya*, the sphere of the manifestation of the Lord. They only last as long as the "mental" element of man in the time of the person as well as in the time of the universe. Beyond is the *Brahman*, the Real and Absolute in oneself, the one and only Truth, which no cultural act could achieve or move, which no austerity could obtain, which no thought could discover.

The spiritual Hindu is he who knows that, the *tadvid*. But to know that does not simply mean having read it in the scriptures or having heard it from the lips of one's guru, nor even of being able to hold forth about it in a learned manner. The true spiritual person is only he who has worked this essential conviction into his life and who has decided to free himself from the world of *maya*, whatever the price he has to pay — the "pearl" of the Evangelist, the price of which is nothing even if one has to give all for it. Doubtless one feels quite comfortable in this world of *maya*, with worship appropriate to the ordinary needs of the soul, with a seductive religious imagery, a reasonably severe but tempered morality, the perspective at last of an agreeable stay in the heaven of the gods, and even an indefinite return to earth for those who wish it. But he who has understood, he can no longer be content with that. He has but one desire, which is to leave all that; for him it is a fire which sears him. He must at all costs follow his path to the Real, in the final solitude, going beyond rites, going beyond all that is symbolic and all mythology, beyond even the teachings pronounced and transmitted in the Veda concerning this Real. An arduous path, perhaps, a dark path of stripping away, reaching ever more unfathomable depths in the bosom of his own being,

> ... for the transcendent path
> is not attainable without pain to mortals!
> (Bhagavad Gita XII, 5)

... Mystical India is not interested in a beyond in the sphere of the Universe, a heaven more or less set in space where reigns a God-monarch surrounded by a court of angels and saints and intervening at leisure in our world. It is in the interior of the real center of this sphere — of the universe, the beyond through the within, opposite of the beyond through the without, but just as "ineffable" — that the spiritual Hindu places (if one dare say "to place") the real God stripped of all attributes, of all multiplicity of forms and of all names.... The sage who formed India lived in the present, his preoccupation not being to materialize in an unforeseeable future; all it is about for him is himself to materialize in his eternal present, is to discover his own being in the eternity of the present instant.

The presentation of the Christian message must in all necessity, to be any use, have integrated first of all this fundamental particular of Indian religious intuition — we speak of intuition and not of its philosophical or theological conceptualizations, still less of the pantheistic deviations which it does not always escape. Otherwise, as high and marvelous as it appears to those who preach it, the Christian message inevitably appears to the Hindu as at a lower level than the *nama rupa,* of the world of names and forms, of the world of manifestation, of *maya*. It will immediately be classed at the same level as the mythological stories of the *Puranas;* the worship proposed will be put in the ranks of the innumerable cults already known in India. Doubtless there will be seen an undeniable usefulness in its order, a "provisional" value at the very least for minds formed at the very center of the culture in which they themselves developed, the Westerners for example. But the value in the order of the Real and the Absolute, a saving value properly so called, no one would ever think of attributing to it, no more real efficacy either, still less unique, in the quest for this Real.

The values of the "within" are certainly not absent from the religion of Christ. Should one not rather say, still more so, that they are the essential constituent? Was not the revelation of Jesus essentially the *interiorization* of the messianic expectation of the Jewish people:

> Is it really at this time, Lord, that You will raise up the kingdom of Israel?

It is not for you to know the time chosen by the Father....

Do not take so many useless cares upon yourselves; one thing alone is important: you will receive the Spirit....

If a person loves me, he will keep my word, my Father will love him. We will come to him and we will make in him our dwelling place. (John 14)

These values of the within have not remained, thank God, simply latent in Christianity. Throughout the centuries, the souls of the mystics have inherited them, resident in the "depths," each one translating his unique experience in the way appropriate to his own culture and according to his own standing. Theologians also came. When by divine grace they too penetrated the within, they learned to bring this mystery of the depths into their great syntheses, at least as much as is possible to man.
— "Initiations à la spiritualité des Upanishads,"
extract from *Guhantara*, Editions Présence, 1979, 41–47

*Abhishiktananda's interest in the liturgy and the ritual of his adopted country bore fruit in many ways. Not only did it increase and deepen his personal understanding, but it led to the incorporation of elements of the Hindu tradition in the worship at Shantivanam, from where this practice has begun to spread to the West. Over time he introduced readings from Hindu religious writings such as the Vedas, the Upanishads, and the Bhagavad Gita, sang Sanskrit and Tamil bhajans (hymns) and used the ancient Hindu blessing arati, when a light is waved before the holy objects and then taken around the congregation, with each of the worshipers putting their hands to the flame and carrying the light of Christ to their eyes. When describing these experiences, for reasons perhaps of modesty or discretion, he often refers to himself as "Vanya."*

## MORNING WORSHIP

The liturgy unfolded. Seated as a choir, the children of the Vedic school sang the Upanishads, the *rudraprasna* of the Yajur veda, Shankara's hymn to Shiva Dakshinamurti and finally the *Upadesa Saram,* a Sanskrit composition by Sri Ramana himself.

During this time a continuous procession wound its way around the venerated tomb. Each new arrival religiously made the circle, always keeping the monument on his right, *pradakshina* — once around, three times around, seven times around. Some people had even vowed to complete this ritual circling 108 times each day. Each time that they passed and repassed the *linga*, which dominates the *samadhi,* they prostrated themselves on the ground in worship and supplication.

Meanwhile within the chancel the priests were busy with their own ritual, as little aware of the children's singing as they were of the movements of the faithful. Each one has his own role to play in worship as in life, and these roles do not interfere with one another. On the sacred stone of the *linga* the priests were continuously pouring out the water of purification, clarified butter, milk, coconut juice, and after each libation, washing the stone and wiping it dry once more. They offered petals of flowers to the rhythm of their litanies of the 108 names of Shiva. They encircled it with garlands of silk and of flowers. They blessed it and offered the cake made of rice, which would later be distributed as *prasada*. Finally they circled the flaming oil lamps while the incense smoke swirled heavenwards.

At this moment the rhythm of the singing slowed down; the chanting rose to the third tone and everyone stood up folding their hands in the *anjali*. As the singers intoned the OM, which brings to an end the Vedic recitation, all the folded hands were raised to face level and on above the heads and soon everyone was lying prostrate on the earth — the highly symbolic gesture by which India expresses her intimate experience of the divine transcendence and her total abandonment to him whom she has recognized.

Meanwhile one of the priests had offered the final *arati*, the camphor flame. He had murmured the usual mantras, but the sound had been lost in the noise of the bell ringing in his left hand and even more in the boom of the temple gong resounding in the vaulted granite roof. He then emerged from the chancel carrying the brass plate on which the flame was burning itself out. Each of the faithful approached and stretched out his hands respectfully over the flame. With his palms thus sanctified by the sacred touch, each one touched his own eyes and then taking a pinch of the holy ash reverently marked his forehead.

Thus ended the morning worship, which always follows the same pattern and is exactly as it was when it was inaugurated many years ago in the lifetime of the Maharishi. Vanya never failed to be present at it when he lived at Tiruvannamalai. For him it was all so deeply meaningful; the place, the memories, the young Brahmins with their long black locks and white *dhotis* and with their foreheads and bare chests marked with lines of ash — just as "Bhagavan" was in his childhood and even when he first came to Arunachala. There was the rhythmic incantation of the Vedic texts and above all there was the Presence — that of the sage, who had lived in this very place for so many long years, and of the mystery which had dazzled him and which had shone first so strongly from him. It was a Presence which enveloped and hung over everything. It seemed to penetrate to the most intimate part of one's being, gathering one into the depths of oneself and drawing one irresistibly within.  — *Guru*, 17–19

## EVENING WORSHIP

One should perhaps recall the fact that for the Hindu the two most sacred hours of the day are still the same as in the most ancient Christian tradition: the mysterious hours of the "meeting" between the night — or day — which is ending and the day — or night — which is beginning, the moments which precede and follow sunrise and sunset.

From the first light the Brahmin is to be found standing in the river waiting for the mystic hour. If there is no river nearby, he will at least have placed a vessel of pure water at his side. Water is in fact the "witness" present at every ceremony and can even take the place of an image if one is not available. The Brahmin takes his bath, recites his mantras especially the *gayatri*, performs the ritual sprinkling of his head, forehead, ears, eyes, each sensory organ, each part of the body, as if performing the rite of consecration and offering the elemental water to the gods — *devas* — who are supposed to preside over the various functions of life. He turns towards the four points of the compass, folding his hands to venerate the devas who protect them. He throws the water out in the four principal directions and immerses himself three times in the water, closing the orifices of his face with his fingers. Finally, as the sun tips the horizon, reaches its fullness, and sweeps up into the sky, he raises his hands joining them above his head and prostrates in the magnificent Hindu gesture of adoration.

Only those whose souls have remained totally insensitive to the mystery of the "holy lights," a mystery both inner and cosmic, and to this marvelous epiphany of God in his creation, would think of labeling such rites idolatrous. This epiphany unfolds in accordance with the rhythm of time — or one might say more truly perhaps that, as it continues to unfold, it introduces this same time factor into a man's being in correspondence with the rhythm of infinite divine freedom. In fact no other country has been so intensely aware as India of the Presence — an eminently active Presence, the whole world of the divine *Shakti,* something resembling the *shekinah* of traditional Judaism. India has felt this Presence since the earliest Vedic era, a presence which is inherent in each being that comes from the hands of the Creator, and in every phase of the life of man and the universe, the daily, monthly, and yearly cycles each of which depends on the phases of the heavenly bodies in which spiritual and uncreated Light manifests itself materially for the benefit of men.

The mystery of Light is thus interwoven in the mystery of water: water from which, as the Vedas say, fire is born: purifying, life-giving water: water which, according to the symbolism of Genesis, was there when life began and which Christianity has honored in the sacrament of regeneration.

In India the act of taking a bath is not simply a matter of hygiene any more than it was at Qumran. Particularly for the Brahmin it is truly an act of worship. Are there in fact any purely secular acts in the life of man? The exacting ritual of the Brahmin is a continuous reminder that nothing is profane. Taking a bath and all forms of ablution are in fact a life-giving contact with the original primary water, the matrix of creation, and this takes place most especially at the moment of vital renewal when the sun reappears. Among the Brahmins of Tamil-Nadu in particular there is no special word to describe ceremonial water: all water is pure and the word they use is *tirtham,* or holy water.

The rite of welcoming the day has its counterpart in the evening rite of farewell, the liturgical entrance into the ambivalent mystery of the night. Both of them stem from traditions transmitted from age to age and stretching back into primeval times when the rite celebrated on earth was considered a necessary element for the stability of the cosmos and regularity of the seasons. It was thought that in the rites of *sandhya,* the discontinuity and disharmony of day and night, of times of sleep and times of waking were reabsorbed and time received an element of permanence and "continuity" both in man and in the universe. — *Guru,* 54–56

## NIGHT PRAYERS

When they were tired of singing and conversing, they quietly stretched out under the *pandal* and dropped off to sleep. Murugan Das continued his songs and litanies long after the others, and, as if echoing his invocations to Murugan, other ejaculations soon broke the silence. The rhythm and intonation strangely resembled those of Tamil Christian worship. Surprised, Vanya listened carefully. There was no doubt that "Our Fathers" and "Ave Marias" were endlessly following one another, punctuated by ejaculations to Murugan uttered by a neighbor. This continued for a long time. Gradually however the rhythm slowed down, the voices became weaker and finally all that could be heard were single invocations at increasing intervals. "YESUVI [Jesus]! ANDAVARE [Lord]! MURUGA TAYARE [Mother]! MARIYAYE [Mary]!"...then at last all were enveloped in the deep silence of sleep. — *Guru*, 116

*Abhishiktananda met Ramana Maharshi only twice — he was not strictly speaking his guru. But one could not be living in an ashram in India without having views on the nature of the relationship between guru and disciple. This is an entry in Abhishiktananda's* Spiritual Diary, *several years before he met the swami who was to become formally his guru.*

## CHRIST THE *SAD-GURU* (TRUE MASTER)

The Hindu goes to God through a guru. As a rule people find the way to God only with the help of someone who has already trodden it, who knows it, not by hearsay, but by personal experience. Direct calls of Grace, as in the case of Ramana Maharshi, remain the exception. The Hindu will explain such cases by going back to the sage's previous life: he had then come to such a stage that no further preparation was necessary in the present life.

The Vedas themselves and all the writings of the masters are only approaches. The first task of the guru was traditionally to recite them to his disciple. Thanks to writing, the aspirant himself is now capable of reading them for himself. But reading is not enough; hearing is mandatory. In both cases it is a matter of a *sruti*, something heard from the One who reveals, and passed on by word of mouth, from generation to generation. One who aspires to the Christian priesthood according to Canon Law must receive the sacred doctrine from a master and may not content himself with learning it from books. So the guru must first recite the Veda, then explain the Veda and especially the *mahāvākyas*.[1] But that is only the external work of the guru. The true guru, precisely because he has "realized," is able to penetrate the soul of his disciple. The whispering of the sacred mantra into the ear of the disciple on the day of his initiation is the symbol of a mysterious and effective whispering from heart to heart. The disciple is connected to God by his guru, not in the sense that the guru would be an intermediary between disciple and God. It is in the person of the guru that God appears to the disciple.

The guru is for the disciple a genuine divine revelation; so the only true guru is one who has "realized...."

My *sad-guru* is Christ Abhishiktesvara. He is the Way, the Truth, and Life. He is the gate of the sheep. No one has seen the Father but the one who came down from the Bosom of the Father.[2] No one has "realized" God as he did. No one has ever been able to have like him the sense of the divine Conscious-

---

1. The great words or central phrases of the Upanishads, such as: "I am Brahman," "That art Thou."
2. Cf. John 14:6; 10:7; 1:18.

ness. "The Father and I are one" [John 10:30]. regarded at the same time as in *dvaita* and in *advaita*.[3] Christ is the Master Guru. Like every true guru he feels an infinite compassion for his disciples.

He lives only for his disciples: "on their behalf I consecrate myself" [John 10:30].

I give myself to Christ as to my *sad-guru*. I "believe" in him, I believe in his worth as Guru and I surrender myself absolutely to him.

How shall I receive his teaching? Two ways:

—the external way of the word,
—the internal way of the Spirit.

His teaching has been handed down to me by successive generations of his disciples. I read it in the Gospel, not to speak of Christian tradition. "He who hears you hears me" [Luke 10:16].

In a deeper sense my guru lives in me by his Spirit. His Spirit he has handed on to me, his *parama-atman*; my guru's *atman* is mine. But first take the theme "Spirit" in the Western sense, spirit of sonship, of piety, wisdom, etc. He is in me in that he passes on to me his "way" of living, of understanding God, realizing God, etc. He is in me in that he shares with me his peace, grace, non-duality [*santam, sivam, advaitam*]. He has kept for himself nothing of what the Father gave him, he has repeated it all, given it all. And finally he has given himself.

He has made us share in his own *tavam*, in his Sonship, in which everything has its origin. He has given us his Spirit. His disciple issued from the water and the Spirit.

---

3. That is, under the aspects of duality and of non-duality.

They have really come back from the great abyss, and received heart, a new spirit. And in Him as in them the whole world is saved from the great abyss, the great waters of death.

My guru's death has freed him in a sense from his own *ahamkara;* in his resurrection he is reborn as the *aham* of all creation.

My *sad-guru* is also present to me in a more mysterious way in the sacrament that resulted from his death and resurrection.

By means of the sacramental rite, those of his disciples who have received authority for it in the name of the community make him present in the midst of the community.

A presence in the form of food, bread and wine. In the form of what can be absorbed, in the form of pure gift, of what is totally, essentially given, handed over.

For my guru is essentially one who is "Given." By giving himself he realized God. And the essence of his teaching will also be about giving oneself, about loving. "There is no greater love than to give one's life for one's friends." "Love one another as I have loved you." "By this all will know...."

So I make him present in the form of a gift, and I receive him who is pure Gift in the form of what is absorbed, and I absorb him, in the form of food, and I eat him.

And this rite at the same time realizes my union with him and is the supreme act of praise offered to the Father and to Him.

—April 3, 1952, *Diary,* 31–33

## MEETING THE GURU

*In 1956 Abhishiktananda heard of a holy man known as Sri Gnanananda, who was known as "the holy man of Tirukoyilur." He was believed to be 120 years old, and incredible stories were told about him. Abhishiktananda traveled with a friend to*

*Tirukoyilur to see him and wrote at length about the experience, which he found to be an "overwhelming encounter."*

The guru, Sri Gnanananda, was sitting in a corner on the far side on a rickety old couch. He had short legs and his body was half shrouded in an orange *dhoti,* which left one shoulder bare, while one end was draped over his head. He was unshaven. On his smooth forehead there was no trace of his 120 years! — only the three lines of ash worn by the devotees of Shiva and the vermilion mark in the center. But from this deeply peaceful face shone eyes filled with immense tenderness.

The visitors greeted him with folded hands but did not prostrate nor even make the slightest gesture of touching the master's feet. Europeans always feel a certain repugnance with regard to these gestures of homage, which are so customary in India and just as natural as genuflecting or kissing the hand in other places.

A carpet was brought and they both sat down. Vanya pushed his friend in front. After all, it was he who had a message for the Swami.

Harold began the conversation, speaking of Govinda Pillai and giving his greetings. He then went on to ask some questions concerning his queries, his "doubts," to use common parlance, about the spiritual life. Krishnamurti translated Harold's questions into Tamil and the guru's replies into English. This quickly became extremely interesting. But the more interesting it became, the more the poor interpreter was out of his depth. He was however a fervent and intelligent disciple. Each evening after his work he used to come to the guru and do everything he could to help him. He would spend the night at the ashram and the next morning would return across the Pennar to his office. The following year he paid for his faithfulness with his life. The Pennar was in flood but nevertheless he was determined to cross and began to wade. The flood water rose out of his depth before he reached the other bank and he was swept away by the current.

There was no doubt about his having a good grasp of English, but the English required for the B.A. of Madras University is more suitable for science and commerce than for philosophy and mysticism! That day Krishnamurti was visibly struggling to cope with subjects that were beyond him. Gnanananda was well aware that the translation was not all it might have been, so he kept on trying to explain in new ways, but the result was only to land the poor interpreter in greater and greater difficulties.

Vanya soon joined in the conversation, first through the medium of English and then directly in Tamil. His Tamil was very elementary and his pronunciation lamentable. Yet soon there developed an understanding in depth between him and the master which was beyond the words being uttered or heard.

After a little while he asked, "What is Swami-ji's position concerning supreme reality? Is it *dvaita* or *advaita?* When all is said and done does any difference remain between God and creatures? For instance is it possible for man to enjoy God and eternally partake of this joy — or is there finally, beyond everything, only being, non-dual (*advaita*) and indivisible in unlimited fulness?

"What is the use of such questions?" replied Sri Gnanananda quickly. "The answer is within you. Seek it in the depths of your being. Devote yourself to *dhyana,* meditation, beyond all forms the solution will be given you."

The visitor then tried again. "Does Swami-ji perform rites of initiation?" In Vanya's mind this was a test question. He knew the love of Hindus for such things and perhaps they are not alone in this? By means of more or less elaborate ceremonies the disciple puts himself under the guru's protection. The latter then secretly transmits to him a mantra which he must faithfully repeat and sometimes adds some rite that must be observed. The disciple is led to believe that he will make wonderful progress by the quasi-"magical" power of this "sacrament," and that he will profit enormously both spiritually and temporally if he repeats the mantra and fulfils the rite. In fact the disciple's faith, if not the guru's grace, does often make effective the initiation — *diksha* — that he has received. The swamis vary considerably in their intentions: some really want to help their disciples, while others want only to extract from them a generous offering or *gurudakshina*. Very often the swami's haste in giving a mantra can only be matched by the incredible alacrity of the disciple in demanding one. Even the well-known disciple of Sri Ramana, Ganapati Sastri, deeply regretted that his master would not agree at least to give mantras to beginners and even suggested he might do so on behalf of his master. For this reason Vanya was awaiting Gnanananda's reply with great interest. "What is the use of initiation?" came the reply. "Either the disciple is not ready, in which case the so-called initiation is no more than empty words, or else the disciple is ready and then neither words nor signs are necessary. The initiation then happens spontaneously."

After a pause he continued, "As long as the world is perceived, there is ignorance, non-wisdom, *a-jnana*. When nothing in the world is any longer perceived, there is wisdom, *jnana*, the only true knowledge."

At this point the devotees began to arrive. Men, women, children, prostrated themselves respectfully, even affectionately. One could easily see that for them this was no empty conventional gesture or rite enjoined by good manners. Quite obviously the bodily prostration revealed the far deeper prostration happening ceaselessly in the secret place of the heart. One saw faith, love, and complete confidence in this man who had become for them nothing less than the epiphany of the invisible Presence, the outward manifestation to their human eyes of the grace and love of the Lord who dwells undivided both in the highest heavens and in the deepest depth of the heart.

The two Europeans were afraid they might be in the way. They asked permission to withdraw. They would go and have a meal in the town, visit the temples, and return later. The guru agreed, but did not want to allow them to leave without offering them a glass of milk. — *Guru,* 23–26

## GREETING THE GURU

If the newest arrival was a man, he would be wearing the usual *dhoti* with his body bare from the waist upwards. First of all he placed his offering at the Swami's feet, stepped lightly backwards, put his hands together in the *anjali,* prostrated himself flat on the ground with his arms above his head, and then touched the floor with his forehead, each ear, and each shoulder. He would then raise himself onto his knees or even stand up, put his hands together once more, prostrate himself full length again and continue, three, five, seven times according to the fervor of his devotion. It is bad manners to prostrate only once and also an obvious sign that one is not high caste. Finally the man would stand up for the last time, cover his ears with the palms of his hands, bow low, touch the master's feet, and then touch his own eyes with the fingers that had been in contact with the revered body of the guru.

The women did not make a full prostration but contented themselves with kneeling down and touching the floor with their foreheads. Sometimes a whole family came together, and the conversation died down while people respectfully watched father, mother, and each child performing the rite one after another.

When the time came to leave, the performance was repeated but this time each person received a piece of fruit or a flower from the pile of offerings which had accumulated. This is known as *prasada* and the faithful received it with both hands, and then reverently touched their eyes with it. Prasada is in fact every grace from above and also every sign of that grace. In particular, after the *pujas* in the temple, it is the return to the faithful of what has been ritually offered. So how could prasada not be in a very special way the gift and the sign of grace, when it is received from the hand of a saint or man of God, for they are more luminous manifestations of the divine and infinite presence than other mortals. The guru's prasada is always received prayerfully, whether it is a leaf, a petal, or a few crumbs of cake, and is then taken home to be shared with the family.

The children quickly realized that prasada was given at the farewell prostration. As a result there were always some little mischiefs who managed to make ritual entrances and departures practically continuously. The guru just smiled and always gave them something as long as an orange or banana remained.

— *Guru*, 35–36

## THE EFFECT OF MEETING SRI GNANANANDA

Vanya had approached this man almost as a tourist and, lo and behold, he had taken possession of his very being, of Vanya. He realized that the allegiance which he had never freely yielded to anyone in his life was now given automatically to Gnanananda. He had heard tell of gurus, of the irrational devotion shown to them by their disciples and their total self-abandonment to the guru. All these things had seemed utterly senseless to him, a European with a classical education. Yet now his very moment it had happened to him, a true living experience tearing him out of himself. This little man with his short legs and bushy beard, scantily clad in a *dhoti*, who had so suddenly burst in upon his life, could now ask of him anything in the world, even to set off like Sadashiva, a dumb and naked wanderer forever, and he, Vanya, would not even think of asking him for any sort of explanation.

Without even considering the matter Vanya and Harold found themselves on the ground pressing the master's feet with fervent hands. — *Guru*, 27

*Another account of the significance of the meeting is found in Abhishiktananda's diary as he struggled to reconcile the flesh-and-blood guru he has just met with Christ, his beloved sad-guru.*

## CHRIST AS GURU

The two encounters of last year must surely have been providential. Neither of them was sought. Whatever may be the value in Christ and then of Dr. Mehta's[4] revelations and of Gnanananda's *sahaja* ["natural" state of realization], I was "led" along that path. And in any case the essential received in both instances is valid. Here is no place for anguish in one who is totally *surrendered*. The sign of full surrender is precisely the radiant peace, the equability, *samatva* that is so evident in my guru (Sri Gnanananda). And in the Lord Jesus, the *sad-guru*, first of all. Posing as a "victim" only shows that the surrender is incomplete. *Samatva* in thought, word, deed....

Why agonize over saying Mass? Say it in all simplicity and if one day I no longer have to say it, leave it unsaid with the same simplicity, the same equanimity.

Why oppose Christ and my guru? Is my guru not the very form under which Christ presents himself to my senses, to my

---

4. Dr. Mehta was a Parsi doctor who had recently been, in a curious way, Abhishiktananda's teacher.

eyes, to my ears, for my prostration, in order to help me reach himself, in the depth of my soul, where he is, which he is in truth?

Christ is more truly close to me in my guru than in any memory I may have of his appearance on earth. The meeting with the guru is truly an epiphany....

The Christ of memory and of faith; Christ manifested in the guru of flesh — these exist with a view to the inner manifestation, the encounter, the recognition.

—January 14, 1955, *Diary*, 139

*The relationship of the guru and the disciple is much misunderstood in the West and so is rejected, even sometimes mocked. At its best and purest this is a truly wonderful relationship whose aim is to impart the highest knowledge and understanding. Most importantly, the guru knows, as is said in the Katha Upanishad, that the disciple "cannot be taught by one who has not reached him; and he cannot be reached by much thinking. The way to him is through the Teacher who has seen him." The one who becomes a guru speaks only from experience; then an extraordinary bond can develop between them. Now Abhishiktananda knew from his own experience what a true relationship with a guru can be.*

## THE MYSTERY OF THE GURU

Beyond the experience of things and places, of watching or of reading or meditating on the scriptures, participating in rites, experience of meeting with or of attending lectures, there is the experience of meeting with men in whose hearts the Invisible has revealed himself and through whom his light shines in perfect purity — the mystery of the guru.

The ancient title "guru" is, alas, too often sullied by being used lightly, if not sacrilegiously. No one should use this word, let alone dare to call someone his guru, if he does not himself have the heart and soul of a *disciple.*

In fact it is as unusual to meet a real disciple as it is to meet a real guru. The Hindu tradition is right to say that when the disciple is ready, the guru will automatically appear: only those who are not yet worthy spend their time running after gurus. The guru and the disciple form a couple, a pair of which the two elements attract one another and adhere to one another. With the two poles they exist only in relationship to one another.... A pair on the road to unity.... A non-dual reciprocity the final realization....

The guru is most certainly not some master or professor, or preacher, or spiritual guide, or director of souls who has learned from books or from other men what he, in turn, is passing on to others. The guru is one who has himself first attained the Real and who knows from personal experience the way that leads there; he is capable of initiating the disciple and of making well up from within the heart of his disciple the immediate effable experience which is his own — the utterly transparent knowledge, so limpid and pure, that quite simply "he is."

Is it not in fact true that the mystery of the guru is the mystery of the depth of the heart? Is not the experience of being face to face with the guru that of being face to face with "oneself" in the most secret corner, with all pretense gone?

The meeting with the guru is the essential meeting, the decisive turning point in the life of a man. But it is a meeting that takes place only when one has gone beyond the level of sense intellect. It happens in the beyond, in the fine point of the soul, as the mystics say.

... What the guru says springs from the very heart of the disciple. It is not that another person is speaking to him. It is not that a question of receiving from outside oneself new thoughts which are transmitted through the senses. When the vibrations of the master's voice reach the disciple's ear and the master's eyes look deep into his, then from the very depths of his being, from the newly discovered cave of his heart, thoughts well up which reveal him to himself.

What does it matter what words the guru uses? Their whole power lies in the hearer's inner response to them. Seeing or listening to the guru, the disciple comes face to face with his true self in the depth of his being, an experience every man longs for, even if unconsciously.

When all is said and done, the true guru is he who, without the help of words, can enable the attentive soul to hear the "Thou art that," *tat tvam asi* of the Vedic *rishis;* and this true guru will appear in some outward form or other at the very moment when help is needed to leap over the final barrier. In this sense Arunachala was Ramana's guru.

Suddenly Vanya stopped in the midst of his story and, his heart filled with sadness, continued, "Do you now see why the word of Western preachers so seldom penetrates the Hindu soul? Yet the Christ whom they proclaim is the guru par excellence. His voice resounds throughout the world for those who have ears to hear and, more important still, he reveals himself in the secret cave of the heart of man! But when will their words and life witness convincingly to the fact that not only have they heard tell of that supreme guru but have themselves met him in the deepest depths of their souls?" — *Guru,* 28–29

## THE GURU IN THE DEPTH OF THE HEART

For the Vedantin, there is only one guru, the one who shines, not-born, in the depth of the heart. The "external" guru is only the temporary form taken by the essential guru to make himself recognized, and at the moment of that recognition there is no longer either guru or disciple. In Christianity it is the church — i.e., individuals in the church and those whom God especially brings into contact with himself — that is the manifested guru, the form actualized in space and time which Jesus takes to reveal himself. The Christian guru is never anything but the manifestation of the Lord, and the moment he forgets this he becomes a thief, no longer a *shepherd*. Similarly, the Vedantin guru who retains the least trace of *ahamkara* [turning back on himself] is a false guru. To insist too strongly that Jesus is the only guru in Christianity risks throwing the church overboard. It remains true that the Vedantin, Zen, etc., guru testifies from his own experience, while the Christian guru testifies from that of Jesus. However, once more, this is only a manner of speaking, for the guru who refers to his own experience shows by that very fact that he has missed the experience. Whoever has not disappeared in the light cannot testify to the light. You must surely know the Persian proverb: "No one knows the secret of the Flame...."

The true experience, whether one reaches it by starting from the Upanishads, from Zen, from Christianity, etc., demands first of all drastic purification of the mind and of the self, and this purification is what our age, in every tradition, most urgently needs. The revolt of young people against all our traditions is the Spirit's warning that without such a purification there will be a devastating upheaval in every religious tradition.

— To Mr. and Mrs. Miller,
November 13, 1970, *LS&T,* 161–62

## THE SECRET OF THE GURU

To know the secret of the Guru...openness is necessary, the "valencies" (as in organic chemistry) needed to catch the guru's summons. Too often we project our own dreams upon the guru

whom we await or have before us, and the relationship is distorted. It is only our very pure "formless" depth that can be reflected in the guru. When the heart is free, the guru emerges, and even more the unique light of which the bodily guru is only a ray, but nearer to and at least more easily accessible to our mind and heart. A guru that is found more cheaply is only a pseudo-guru, or at least merely one to take us on a single stage.... Beyond the insipidities and superficialities of ashrams find the deep experience. Discover Arunachala beyond even Ramana, so deep in the heart of Ramana that even the images (bodily, mental, etc.) of Ramana have disappeared, and Arunachala too. Only the Flame, without any bounds. That is where the mystery of Christ is found. Do not diminish him; henceforth he is present in the humblest glance or act of service.
— To a Frenchwoman living as a hermit, *LS&T,* 152

*Another aspect of Indian life in which Abhishiktananda immersed himself was pilgrimage, which in its true sense means a journey to a place believed to be sacred in a specific way. From 1956 Abhishiktananda went on pilgrimages. He went to the temple of Sadashiva Brahman, the eighteenth-century yogi who never spoke a word and wore no clothes at all. He explored every inch of the holy mountain of Arunachala, climbing to the summit and making the ritual circuit of the mountain known as the* giri-pradakshina, *believed to gain great merit for the person who does it. And three times he went on pilgrimages in the Himalayas, the Mecca for all pilgrims in India, to the sources of the Ganges. So in writing about pilgrimage Abhishiktananda was, as one comes to expect from him, writing from experience.*

## PILGRIMAGE — A DEFINITION

[Pilgrimage] is the universal response of man to the call which comes from the hills whose summits he instinctively connects with the dwelling place of God, his Creator. And irresistibly he returns there as if to the source of his being. Down from those heights flow both the streams which water the earth and also those mystical rivers to which souls come to find the water of life. —*Mountain*, 137

## SETTING OFF

People of all conditions and ages are to be seen. Children, babies in arms, old men leaning on their sticks, old women bent double and dragging themselves along, they are all there. You see the *babus*, the important people, too. The latter travel on the backs of mules, followed by their servants and an army of coolies, who carry either on their shoulders or slung by a strap from their foreheads the ample baggage deemed indispensable! The wives and children of the *babus* are carried on litters or in baskets on the coolies' backs. But it is the poor and the humble, those whom the Gospel terms blessed, who form the great mass of this continuous procession which winds its way up the Ganges. With bare feet or shod in ill-fitting sandals, a staff in hand, a bundle slung over the shoulder or on the woman's head, they set off, their eyes glued to the path, suffering from the rigors of the way, but filled with joy and with the Lord's name continually on their lips.

At night they halt at the *dharamshalas*, the caravanserais of India. At one of the few shops and at a price which increases at each succeeding stage of the journey, they buy a little flour, rice, or lentils, gather up a few sticks, make a fire between two stones, and cook a meal. Then they stretch out where they can in caravanserais which are always full, wrapping themselves up as best they can in their poor clothes, for the cold is severe at that height, especially for people who are used to the burning sun of the plains. Thus they rest for a few hours before setting off again to have the *darshan* of the Lord high up in his sanctuary.

Often one hears a group of women taking up a song, or perhaps a refrain, or even a single phrase indefinitely repeated to a haunting rhythm. Shiva, Rama, Krishna, the names ring out from the heart, and the pilgrim, praying and singing and thinking of God, forgets all the fatigue of the way. Meanwhile the men devote themselves to theology. Among the pilgrims there is always someone who has read a bit more than most people and who would feel very selfish if he kept his knowledge to himself. His fellow pilgrims generally listen to him with great attention, answer his questions, approve, discuss, and ask for more explanations. This often lasts for hours. Only late at night do the replies become less frequent, shorter, eventually being reduced to a few inarticulate monosyllables, while the speaker himself continues tirelessly and always at the top of his voice, without a thought for the drowsiness of his listeners, until at last he in his is turn is overcome by sleep and fatigue.

Then at last the great silence is punctuated only by the breathing of the sleeping pilgrims, by the crying of ejaculatory prayers of those who do not manage to wake in the night. "OM Shiva, Shiva" murmurs one: "OM Krishna, Krishna" intones another.... — *Mountain*, 141–42

## ASCENT TO GANGOTRI

Some years later I made the ascent to Gangotri.

This time I was with the pilgrims for it was the month of June, which is the height of the season for pilgrims. I was following up the Bhagirathi on the steep stony paths, my pack on my back and bamboo staff in hand, exchanging with those whom I met the traditional salutation to the Ganges, the Alma Mater, or more often answering them with the one word OM, which, in the mountains, is the traditional greeting given to the *sadhu* and expected from him in reply. In fact is not OM the mantra par excellence, if not the unique mantra of the true *sadhu* and most especially of the pilgrim *sadhu*? All along the way is it not OM which wells up from his heart as it wells up from the river, the mountain, the forest, and from every living being met on the way? This OM, which breaks forth from the roar of the Ganges, from the rustling of leaves, from the twittering of the birds and echoes indefinitely across the sheer cliff faces, is the OM which wells up in the pilgrim's heart like an infinite echo repeating itself, increasing and finally merging into the primordial OM in the silence in which all is said. All along the way the pilgrim *sadhu* murmurs with the lips the OM which springs up from his heart. He quietly chants it when he is not too tired. He even makes an effort to pronounce it in order to forget his fatigue. And when he meets other pilgrims he has only to say it a little louder to acknowledge their greeting and bless them in the name of God. — *Mountain*, 151–52

## *SADHUS*

Along the way the *sadhus* have their own rhythm and their rites to perform. They are never in a hurry like other pilgrims. Is not their life a perpetual pilgrimage, in winter along the roads in the plains, in summer along mountain paths, from village to village, from temple to temple, from pilgrimage to pilgrimage? In the morning, when most people's thoughts go first to a bowl of tea to prevent them from freezing, the *sadhus* go off to some spring or neighboring stream to bathe in the icy water. Then they return to the *dharamshala* for their mantras and meditation. Only after that will they leave, often in a group. If they have a few coins they will cook for themselves on reaching the next halting place; if not, some pilgrim will give them a little food as alms. In the evening, when others are singing or have already fallen asleep, they continue with their prayers, sometimes in front of an icon which they carry carefully at the bottom of their bag and place respectfully in front of them on the floor between two sticks of incense to offer him their worship.

— *Mountain,* 145–46

## THE COSMIC COVENANT

Hinduism belongs to the "Cosmic Covenant." This term is now commonly used by Christians to refer to all the religious experiences of mankind apart from biblical revelation. Cosmic religions essentially consist in the worship of God as he manifests himself in nature, and reach their highest point in contemplating him in the deepest center of the heart. From the dawn of history they have established a sacred meeting-point between man and his Creator, and even the special revelations which came later had to build upon the basis of that cosmic encounter. The cosmic covenant does not emerge only at one particular stage of man's civilization or cultural development. Rather it is written into the very nature of things and is embedded in the consciousness of mankind. Every man discovers something of it, even if confusedly, the moment he awakes to and becomes present to himself, to the world, and so to God. Some men, endowed with a greater capacity for spiritual things, and more particularly aided by divine grace, penetrate more deeply into the mystery and unveil its secret to their brothers. These are the prophets and seers, who never fail to make their appearance wherever the desire for God is wholehearted and pure. And yet no prophet or seer of the cosmic covenant has ever received or taught anything substantially new. All was given from the beginning; his task is only to recognize that which is and to decipher more and more of its mystery.

...*Sanatana dharma*, the eternal law, the religion that has no beginning, is the traditional name of what is commonly known as Hinduism. It is certainly one of the loftiest expressions of the cosmic covenant. The advaitic experience, which is the heart of Hinduism, is beyond question the highest point attainable by man in the contemplation of the mystery of man and nature. It has been supremely successful in both integrating and transcending the myths which are the necessary milieu of religions. The cosmic religions in fact originate, develop, and are transmitted in and through myth, and yet the myth which bears them needs to be continually renewed and transcended if it is not to cause inflexibility and stagnation. Vedanta does not renounce myth but, while probing it to its very source, keeps it under control and uses it to lead man to his own final mystery. Most followers of the cosmic religions are satisfied with the manifestations of divinity or of the sacred in the forms and forces of nature.

But India, at least in her seers, allows herself no respite until she has unraveled its ultimate secret, the very mystery of *Brahman*,[5] as she calls it. India pursues this mystery into the deepest level of man's consciousness. There she finds both the source and the consummation of all that is, and attains to the complete satisfaction of every wish, the perfect peace and final bliss which is her heart's desire. Yet at the very moment of this discovery all forms disappear, worship is muted into silence, all praise and all petition are seemingly transcended, all *bhakti* and all *karma* apparently come to an end.

—*Saccidananda*, 52–54

*Abhishiktananda had become as much an Indian as he was a Frenchman — indeed he had taken Indian nationality and was*

---

5. The Absolute Being, omnipresent and transcendent.

*never again to return to his native France. So Indian had he become that sometimes he wrote as if he were a Hindu addressing Christians, as in the following two pieces — a tongue-in-cheek unpublished review of one of his own books and an article that he wrote with his friend Murray Rogers.*

## REVIEW OF *HINDU-CHRISTIAN MEETING POINT*

Reading this book with the critical but nevertheless sympathetic eyes of a Hindu, I cannot but rejoice sincerely that at long last some Christians are coming to appreciate and understand our Hindu spiritual experience.

Like most Westerners, Christians came here as plunderers. They tried to remove from our souls the treasures which were lying and fructifying there from time immemorial. But those treasures were enshrined too deeply in the hearts of the sons of Bharat to be altogether lost. Life can be snatched away or even surrendered freely, but that Source of Life is beyond all threats or destruction....

It was difficult, of course, for them to realize that far from guarding jealously such treasures, we have no dearer desire than to share them with anybody who is worthy of receiving them, that means, who is willing to approach our masters with the dispositions explained in our sastras [Vedic Scriptures], viz., discrimination, humility, and equanimity of mind, a spirit of renunciation and a true longing for salvation.

As rightly recognized by the author of the book, our treasure is, first and foremost, *brahmavidya,* the knowledge of the secret hidden in the "cave of the heart," that *guha* of the Upanishads, that highest heaven, abode of Brahman, *nihito guhayam parame vyoman* (Tait.U.2.1). At such a level all competition and rivalry between *dharmas,* or religions are simply transcended, and there all people of good will and genuine spiritual experience can meet together beyond all symbols and without any misgiving.

We Hindus strongly believe that Hinduism, at least once one has gone beyond the external plane of mere religious practices, is a shortcut towards this experience of liberation; in fact most of us maintain that this cannot be attained except when a man at long last has been given the grace of being born as a Hindu and has deserved, through his past good *karma,* to meet in this life a real guru, from whom he will receive the definitive *upadesha*. Yet we cannot but acknowledge and esteem the sincerity of so many religious people whom circumstances of birth have placed outside the fold of the Vedic religion. After all, as long as the ultimate knowledge has not yet shone in the depth of the heart, every thing, at every level, has only the value of sign or symbol. Even at the level of the mind, the supreme truth can simply be adumbrated through myths and concepts — the well-known *darshana* of the star Arundhati. Among religious systems, some may be superior theoretically and according to the scale of values of this world, but, as the Gita strikingly puts it, it is normally better for each one to follow his own *dharma* which, after all, is the one most suitable to the conditions of life in which he has been born. The best *dharma,* we may however say, is the one through the fulfillment of which people come to understand that it is essentially a *path* towards the Transcendent, towards the Reality which is beyond all modes and qualifications.

We realize, naturally, that it is difficult for a Christian to accept that his own Christian *dharma* should be itself transcended. We are familiar of course with that theme which has gained ground among them in the past years, and which appears in this book in many places, that all religions, including Hinduism, are tending, by means of their own spiritual development and under the impulse of the "Holy Spirit," towards

Christ and Christianity as their fulfillment and culmination, and that those who are saved meanwhile even outside the fold of Christianity are saved "implicitly" through Christ and the church. Before Christianity even existed, Sri Krishna Bhagavan had already explained to Arjuna that all worship was really directed towards Himself even when outwardly addressed to any deity of any name whatsoever. As a friend of mine answered a Christian priest who was developing this theory before him: "Father, I agree with you in everything, except for a minor detail. I feel that my master Sri Aurobindo has shown better than any of your theologians that the universe is growing towards a final point, the point Omega as you now say. Only you call that point Christ, whereas I call it Vishnu!"

Again, one of the best Christian theologians of India has unveiled at length in our scriptures and our *darshans* what he calls "the unknown Christ of Hinduism."[6] All he succeeded finally in showing however is that there is nothing in Christianity that we do not already possess one way or another in Hinduism, and that it is irrelevant to quibble as to whether we shall call the "mediator" Christ or Ishvara; actually by equating Christ with Ishvara, he accepts implicitly that Christ belongs to the sphere of *maya*, and that therefore Christianity has only relative value — which is just what we Hindus are constantly pointing out! Is it not clear that such theologians are simply trying frantically to save their own Christian *dharma* from the blinding light which it cannot endure — like a man who tries to blot out the sun in the daytime in order to be able to enjoy the light of the moon! However that may be we rejoice heartily when our Christian brothers get at least some glimpses of that Light. The deeper that awareness penetrates in their hearts, the brighter

---

6. Reference to his friend Raimundo Panikkar's *The Unknown Christ of Hinduism* (London: Darton, Longman & Todd, 1964; rev. ed., Maryknoll, NY: Orbis Books, 1981).

will that Light shine inside and the sooner will the day come when their mind and spirit will be unable to resist its splendor.

The author inevitably has some limitations in his point of view since he is looking at the Hindu experience from the windows of Christianity, but he has exercised care not to use expressions offensive for the Hindu. Indeed he has gone as far as is possible for a believing Christian in the understanding of that experience. At times we are almost expecting him to take the final leap and let himself be taken to that "other bank" of which he speaks so longingly. Alas! His desperate clinging to his own *dharma*, or rather to the external and mental elements of it, cannot but prevent him from reaching "that bank." His limitations are the limitations of his *dharma*, we would say, of any *dharma* which recoils on itself. When Hindus also try to cling to any of their mental concepts or put their trust in mere ritualism, afraid that, otherwise, as someone put it, they will not be able "to taste the sugar," they build by this very fact an insuperable fence between God in His own reality and themselves. It is only naked that man can cross to the "other shore of darkness." It is completely alone that man must be willing to face God, no covering of any kind which would veil him from God or from himself, no help whatsoever from outside to dictate to him his proper attitude in the Presence of the Absolute. Face to face with God, in the solitude of God alone can a man find God and find himself....

Should not all spiritually minded people both from Hinduism and from Christianity, and indeed from all religious traditions of the world, come together at long last and decide that their first work should be to help one another and also their brothers to "convert within" and to find the way to the cave of the heart?

As can be inferred already, we have never believed in a so-called ideal Truth on the model of the platonic ideas, existing in some mythical heaven and therefore capable of being defined in well-framed concepts and of saving anyone who accepts formally those concepts. Truth is living reality. Man cannot reach it except by the supreme commitment of himself, beyond all formulations, all external laws and obligations. Hence the importance we Hindus put on the inner conversion, starting with the religious approach with which anyone is most familiar and then leading him step by step to that inner Mystery of himself and of the Godhead, the indivisible-advaitic-experience of *atman-brahman,* beyond all signs, therefore comprising all signs, making him realize finally that the presence is transcendent to all and immanent to all....

The author of the book has at least indicated the way. May his readers follow the path up to the end and reach the other bank of "the space of the heart."

— Unpublished, in possession of
Father Murray Rogers, date unknown

## HINDU-CHRISTIAN DIALOGUE POSTPONED

Now you want to have dialogue with us. You tell us very nicely that you have to learn from us. You begin to speak a great deal about our scriptures, our traditions, the religious experience of our mystics. There are even in your papers violent controversies on the matter,[7] which amuse us a good deal. Some wonder, however, at your intentions. Is it not true that all Semitic religions, be they Judaism, Islam, or Christianity, are founded on the notion of a chosen people which has received from God directly the mission to convert the whole world to their particular tenets? Do you not realize then that such an approach to the

---

7. A reference to the Bombay Christian weekly *The Examiner,* whose correspondence columns have been full of letters, some sadly emotional, on the use in Christian worship of symbols already used by Hindus.

religious sphere affects immediately all attempts at a real dialogue? You should not be surprised therefore when not a few among us suspect your "stretched out hand" and your so sweet invitation to dialogue, as was put very bluntly in *The Organizer* for instance when the Pope came to Bombay.

You will answer me of course that such superior attitude is not uncommon among us Hindus as well. Bigotry indeed is to be found everywhere, and I wonder sometimes whether it is not a small minority only of believers — in any religion whatsoever — who do not make use of God and of religion simply to assert their own identity. Yet to speak now of religion as it should be I think there is a sharp difference between Christians and Hindus in their very approach to this problem. You at least are acquainted enough with our scriptures to know the Copernican revolution brought to our initial religious approach by the Upanishads, something similar to, but much more radical than the freedom from law and rituals brought by the preaching of Jesus. Our Upanishads may have been interpreted differently by different *acharyas* yet nobody can contest that the Upanishadic seers, taking to their extreme consequences intuitions of the Vedas, have directed the whole Hindu tradition towards the inner Mystery, beyond all forms.

Too often, I know, our Neo-Vedantists do not resist the temptation of making a kind of religion of the advaitic experience, betraying by doing so its real import. But in itself the Vedanta lies at the level of experience, something incommensurable with any kind of rituals, dogmas, or social structures. Therefore, there is no possibility for a claim of superiority from the part of the *Vedanta* in relation to any *dharma*. Vedantic experience and *dharmas* belong respectively to planes which cannot be compared. And as regards the superiority of Hinduism over other *dharmas*, this could at the most be argued only on the phenomenological plane, which means taking into consideration the mentality of the peoples of India. You see how far that is from the absolute claim of superiority on the part of Semitic religions.

But let us come back to our initial point. To allure us to dialogue you keep telling us that we have to learn from each other. Excellent! Without any false pride I confess that we Hindus have already learned a lot from you Christians, on the external level. But do you think sincerely that formal and academic dialogue is the best way to learn? Why all this fuss about well planned and prepared official dialogue? If really you want to learn from us — I mean to learn from us the best we can give you — why not take the traditional Indian attitude of the disciple? Even learned Brahmins, in our Upanishads, did not think it below them to come in such a manner to learn from *kshatriyas*. Go with humility and sincerity to the feet of some real guru, a knower of the scriptures and at the same time a man of personal experience, as the *Mundaka* says. Such a guru will explain to you the inner meaning of the Vedas; he will lead you step by step to that very experience which he himself has obtained by the grace of his own guru. Do not forget that spiritual experience cannot be the object of courses or lectures. Words are necessary of course to prepare the mind, but they can convey the truth only indirectly, for no word can express adequately the Mystery. The Mystery is the object of personal and direct experience only. The teaching of the guru is but a part of the "initiation." Life with him and with the family of his disciples is no less important, as are also worship and silent meditation with him. More than that is the immediate inner contact of the disciple with the guru, at the level of the soul, when at long last his mind is attuned enough. Do you understand now why we remain doubtful of your intentions, or at least of your awareness of the real problem involved when you invite us to learn from each other through formal discussions? *Brahmavidya* is not a matter of discussion, but of initiation, the guru playing rather the role of a catalyst which makes possible the direct contact between the man and the light which shines in his inner self.

I am afraid really that when you call us to dialogue you do not understand spiritual knowledge in the way we do. You want information; you want learned discussions on the phenomenal aspects of religions, those phenomenal aspects ranging from rituals and sociological aspects of it up to mythology and doctrinal formulations. All are things of human interest, I do not deny it, but all remain short of the ultimate — the *parama pada* — which alone really interests the man who has got even a glimpse of the inner Mystery.

*— Practical Anthropology* 18, no. 6
(November–December 1971)

# 5

# The Life of the Hermit

ॐ

*Abhishiktananda had mixed feelings about following the life of the hermit. He was a sociable man, who had many friends and who loved to talk. On the other hand he was, increasingly, called to the life of the hermit, the solitary. He himself was amazed that "a temperament so little fitted as mine for the life of the hermit should have found there a fullness never, never experienced anywhere else."*[1] *Throughout his life in India he spent long periods in solitude, in 1968 retiring to a small hut at Gyansu in the Himalayas, where he spent at least half the year as a hermit. So he lived not only as a* sannyasi, *the one who has renounced, but also as a hermit, spending long long periods in silence and solitude.*

## THE IDEAL OF THE *SANNYASI*

The Spirit blows where he wills. He calls from within, he calls from without. May his chosen ones never fail to attend to his call! In the desert or the jungle, just as much as in the world, the danger is always to fix one's attention upon oneself. For the wise man, who has discovered his true Self, there is no longer

---

1. Letter to Canon Lemarié, April 29, 1953, *Life*, 71.

either forest or town, clothes or nakedness, doing or not-doing. He has the freedom of the Spirit, and through him the Spirit works as he wills in this world, using equally his silence and his speech, his solitude and his presence in society. Having passed beyond his "own" self, his "own" life, his "own" being and doing, he finds bliss and peace in the Self alone, the only real Self, the *parama-atman*. This is the true ideal of the *sannyasi*.

— *Further Shore*, 16

*Abhishiktananda had known about the nature of* sannyasa, *the life of total renunciation, for a long time before he practiced it seriously himself. In fact as early as 1956, at Swami Gnanananda's ashram, he was able to deal with inappropriate personal questions, such as where and when someone was born, in a way which clearly impressed his guru. Once again he refers to himself as "Vanya."*

## *SANNYASA*

Vanya then replied to the importunate *sadhu:* "I am sorry, Maharaj, but these are questions one just does not ask, especially between *sadhus*. There is no sense in them. From the moment a man receives *sannyasa* he ceases to have family, home, or country. A *sadhu*'s home is where he happens to be. If you insist on setting store by such things, is it not nearest the truth to say that his homeland, that is, the place where he was born, where he came from, and where he is going, is the "cave of the heart" of which the scriptures speak? It is the *guha,* or inner cave, into which he is always delving deeper. Is not this ochre robe that covers my body the outward sign that I renounced everything the day I put it on and that I have no longer the right to call a single thing on earth my own? What I was or where I was yesterday or ten years ago is utterly irrelevant. What does it matter where this body was born, or what name was given by those who received the child at birth? The real *sadhu* possesses neither name nor country and should in fact possess no *I*."

Swami Gnanananda was visibly pleased with Vanya's reply. Looking at him but speaking to Shivaprakasham, he added simply: "Why do you ask such questions? He should not even remember the things you are asking him!" — *Guru*, 40

*Abhishiktananda thought and wrote much about surrender — something he knew was essential but which he found extremely difficult, often lamenting his inability to achieve it. He wrote of his anguish at being torn between Christianity and* advaita, *"Surrender both my desire to remain a Christian, born of an instinctive fear, and my desire to live completely as the advaitin Hindu which I often think I am. In total surrender to the mystery. Free and naked at the heart of the abyss, hanging there...."* (Diary *September 5, 1955, 124*).

## SURRENDER

During those feast days, which I formerly lived so intensely as a Christian, how deep is my anguish. I can no longer appreciate anything in them. Whoever has once had the "taste" of *advaita* on his tongue no longer enjoys the flavor of anything else.

However as regards the "surrender," I have not yet managed to achieve it — the "surrender" of my "ego" as a Christian, a monk, a priest. And yet, I must do so. Perhaps it will then be given back to me, renewed. But meanwhile I must leave it behind — totally — without any hope of its return. And that means absolute poverty, nakedness, hunger, fasting, a vagrant life without means of support, total solitude in heart, in body, and in spirit.

And still more, it involves the breaking of all those bonds that are as old as myself, those bonds that are in the most secret recess of the heart. All that superego derived from my family upbringing, from my whole training as a child, as a young man, as a priest, as a monk. Received from others, welling up from myself within myself. — January 6, 1956, *Diary*, 136

*During Abhishiktananda's time with Dr. Mehta he learned about surrender with a touching humility and eagerness.*

Only to the extent that you are not attached to any thought, to any point of view, to anything at all, that you do not desire or fear anything, that you do not feel delight or sorrow in anything — only so can the void be created in your intellect. If I am worried about what will happen tomorrow, about what I will have to decide tomorrow, I will not be able to reach this void. I must have absolute faith in this mystery of the beyond into which I throw myself. Whether I call it Christ, Shiva, Parama-atman does not matter. Total acceptance that someone is there to receive me, to take complete charge of me, or rather that in the end I will find myself set free from all my present limitations. — July 27, 1955, *Diary*, 106–7

*He found that for the surrender to be complete all stability had to be "blown up" and he constantly referred to nakedness, "a nakedness which could perhaps be more accurately called a flaying." Here is not only surrender but an impressive humility.*

I have been "stripped stark naked" in my soul these days in Bombay-Poona. And my "pride" in having realized something has been swept away, and I have been made to understand that everything that I had, not only through my intelligence and through my previous study and meditation, but also everything

# The Life of the Hermit

that I thought I had learned when hidden in the heart of Arunachala, was nothing, nothing at all, simply the babbling of a child....

Here I have to be simply a disciple, and even to receive through this other person the message from him with whom I thought I was one. Great pride in the conviction that one has passed beyond *advaita*, when one has scarcely set foot on the road, entered the stream.    — August 2, 1955, *Diary*, 113

*One of the most moving passages he wrote about surrender comes as a sort of prose poem, a style into which he often broke when words could not contain his thoughts — like this one at the end of* The Further Shore.

## "NAKED AS A STONE IS NAKED"

For "He is" — other than himself; and yet, if he *is*, this
    must be so in his own greatest depth.
The descent into the abyss, where nothing is any more
    seen, not even himself!
Then rising up from the abyss to the Light, and once more
    finding "himself" — the "Passover"!
    "Awakened," I find myself again in Thee,
*resurrexi et adhuc tecum sum.*

And men amuse themselves, excite themselves,
and men make war, make love, make money,
and the learned discuss, and the scribes make rules...
I have seen everything that is done under the sun;
and behold
all is vanity,
said the Preacher.

The descent into hell and the rising again
on the morning of Easter —
For it is necessary to descend to the depths of the abyss
in order to awaken on the Further Shore,
that other side to which in fact there is no "other."
That "Other" which is in my own depths
and to which there is
no "other,"
that is, Being, the Self.

But the Further Shore —
man must come to it all alone,
naked as a stone is naked,
naked as glass is naked,
naked as the self is naked.
He began his work with the sacrament of the Universe,
continued it with the sacrament of humanity,
and completed it with the sacrament of the church.
And in the power of this last sacrament,
man plunged into the abyss.
Through his Faith.
But there he abandoned everything —
all that clothed him, all that adorned him,
all that hid him from himself,
either by enhancing or by cloaking him.
All was snatched away from him —
his body itself by death,
even the joy of feeling himself beloved of God —
*Deus meus, ut quid me dereliquisti?*
Father, why have you forsaken me?

Abandoned by men, and abandoned by God,
alone with himself,
alone, infinitely alone....

There he discovered the aloneness of the Alone,
and the aloneness of Being,
and the joy of BEING, the peace of Being, the freedom
  of Being.

He awoke; there was no longer an abyss, nor a river, nor
  any river-banks,
Arunachala had disappeared,
"He was." ...

And so he reached the Further Shore....

> In this depth of the self,
> where one is, before any foundation was dug,
> or anything was built there
> by human hand or brain,
> and deeper than any shaft that man has dug,
> prior to and deeper than the emergence of any desire,
> prior to and deeper than the emergence of any symbol,
> be it image or idea;
> alone with the self, at the source of its being,
> alone with the Absolute,
> alone in the aloneness of the Alone,
> in the *kevala,* the solitude that has no name,
> there where the spirit issues from the hands of its Creator,
> and outside Him, yet still in Him, awakes to the being
> which Alone He IS.

— From Appendix, Two Poems,
*Further Shore,* 123–25

---

*Solitude and silence swim in the same waters, as close as sisters. Though silence can be maintained in company, they do not mix well, while, for the solitary, silence is an inevitable companion.*

## SILENCE

I was given a wooden hut in an enclosure reserved for *sadhus* on the far side of the spring. I set aside two days for getting to know the people and the geography of the place and then entered the greater silence. I had in fact decided that I would make use of this stay in Gangotri by spending at least a few days as a *muni*. I would only allow myself those signs which are absolutely indispensable. What is more, I had not brought with me a single book. I wanted to experience this interior barrenness which, so I had been told, would reflect more truly the mystery which here enveloped me. I also wished to participate more nearly in the life of my brother *sadhus* and to try through personal experience to make my own what happens in the soul of a *muni* in the interior and exterior silence.

... One day I had gone down close to the bed of the Ganges by a goat path on the far side of the Gaurikund waterfall. Leaning against a pine tree I was quietly watching the river flow by. Then I heard the sound of hands being clapped together as if someone were calling me. As I wished to keep silence I pretended not to hear. However a naked form soon approached and signed to me to follow. I made a sign that I was not speaking.

The naked man signed to me that he was also keeping silence. By more signs he insisted that I follow him. He led me to his hut made of rough wood and branches, being the extension of a cave. He signed to me to sit down on the sand. There in the middle of the hut was a hearth with a wood fire. On a tripod stood a pan containing his dinner. Still by the means of signs he asked if I had had my meal. On my replying in the affirmative he took the pan off the fire and replaced it with a pot into which he poured Ganges water and set it to boil. He crushed up a few grains of pepper which he threw into the water and added tea, sugar, and milk, strained it through an old rag, and invited me to drink the concoction. Surely this was the hospitality of the old monks of Scete and Thebes? Sitting opposite one another on each side of the fire we looked at each other. He showed me the Ganges through a neatly contrived peephole in the rough wall of branches. He gave me to understand that for him the Ganges was everything. Just to look at the river was enough to make him forget everything else. Outside objects, his body, thought, everything disappeared, or so he conveyed to me, when he turned to look at the sacred waters. I came to understand also that there was room in his heart only for peace and joy, a serenity which nothing could disturb, a joy which was complete because it was fulfilled and no desire whatever could henceforth come to disturb his happiness.

Near him lay a bit of broken slate and a chalk. I asked him for them. My Hindi was indeed very poor and poorer when written than spoken. Nevertheless I was interested to know a little more about my host. Thus I came to know that he had lived for twelve years in complete silence dividing his time between Rishikesh and Gangotri. I asked him for his mantra, his prayer. Immediately he wrote down "OM Ganga Mai!" OM Mother Ganges! I noticed how thin his body was, so I asked him if he was not concerned about it and if he would not think of taking some medicine. His immediate reply was full of meaning. He made quick gestures of rolling up invisible sleeves and then with folded hands pointed heavenwards. Indeed what matters this body which passes away and withers like the flower and the grass? When the Lord entrusts it to you, you take the necessary care of it. When he wants it back, you roll it up without a sigh or a moment's regret and shoot up to the Real.

Here indeed was the pure acosmism![2]

---

2. "Acosmic": a word used in ancient Greek Christian literature to describe the monk who lived completely out of the world.

...The true *muni* is he who has no need to talk either within himself or with others. If he still needed to speak to God, to a God whom he still conceived or imagined in some form, even if the form were within himself, what would be the point of being outwardly silent? He would do better to remain with men, to sing in a choir with them. The *muni* is he who has discovered the Transcendent within himself and is no longer capable of being *before* him. "Ah, ah, ah, Lord," as said Jeremiah. *"I cannot speak."* He remains silent. It is finished. And it no longer means anything for him to say, as do the aesthetes of the Transcendent, that he is silent and God indescribable.

— *Mountain,* 152, 155–57

*It is perhaps not surprising that Abhishiktananda should have written often to his sister Thérèse about silence and solitude, for in 1952 she had become a nun at Saint-Michel's, the convent near the monastery where her brother had been a monk for nearly twenty years. These are some extracts from his letters to her.*

Solitude is only worth anything when filled with the presence of the Lord. (1952)

I dream more and more of leading the real life of a *sadhu,* owning nothing other than the *dhoti* which covers the loins and the stole which protects his shoulders, collecting his handful of rice every lunchtime. I dream of having the strength to do it one day. It would be the best New Year's wish I could receive. Free from everything, night of all, silence of all, alone with Alone, who, alone, lives within my solitary heart. (Christmas 1955)

Joy is forever, for it is in the heart where the Lord resides. Think about something being wordless, without trying to feel anything. That which is there within you, deeper than your own heart. Suppress those words between him and you which separate you more than they unite you. Look in silence. It is such a presence. And it lives there in front of you! In that joy of the Presence. (March 1963)

*So too he wrote to her about poverty and about* sannyasa, *the life of renunciation. This letter was written a few months before he died.*

*Sannyasa.* I wanted to be courageous enough to go to the extreme in the clothes I wear, and as I am ashamed of all that is not necessary in the way of clothes, food, conveniences of life. The true *sannyasi* ought not to have anything.... Everything depends on the compassion of the people in the villages through which he passes.

The other day in a Hindu ashram, I met a Christian monk who also lives in total poverty and goes from ashram to ashram, happy all the time, whether he has something to eat or not. Naturally he has no job. He doesn't even have the formal status of *sannyasi,* but he is the most authentic Christian Indian monk I have met, though no one knows him. It is solitary monks such as this who will one day bring about the true Indian Christian monasticism. And I am not talking about the real Hindu monks, most often unknown, who live their ideal to the letter. I dream that I might in the end live my last years as a true hermit.

The harder this is, the sweeter the true cross. I have never been so peaceful in my life as I have since I led this very hard life here. — MT, July 6, 1973, *LS&T,* 3–4

## SOLITUDE

The high peaks are nothing but bare rock. No place is found there for grass or trees. Nothing but solid rock which holds the snows. It is only halfway up that there are trees, birds, and wild animals.

The high peaks stand up starkly against the sky, clothed only in space. Thus too is the monk, naked, alone, motionless.

The solitude of the monk is complete in the very fact of his being at the center of everything and at the highest peak of everything. The flowing river, the tree bursting into leaf, the singing bird, the child playing, the coolie gasping for breath, all are gathered up in the OM which rings in his heart. And all that has ever been and ever will be is the OM which wells up from the depth of his heart.

It is on the true center of all beings that he is fixing his attention when he is concentrating deep within his own heart. It is in fact on the center of the One who is that he is concentrating at that very moment within himself. And, as he gathers up everything within himself, he is bringing it back to its true center.

Such is the aloneness of him who is alone: aloneness which seeks no support, no backing up by anything else at all, which provides no one to appeal to, no one to ask anything from.

Aloneness with God is not the aloneness of God. The aloneness of God is just being alone, absolutely alone, infinitely alone. It is the aloneness of Jesus as He at the very point of death was alone: *Eloi, Eloi, lama sabachthani?* And such is the only way which leads to coming face-to-face with God.

Who, one may ask, will be willing to live in such aloneness? Alone in his own inner solitude? Not with his memories, not with his thoughts or with his books, but alone with himself, stripped of everything. Alone with the single OM which wells up from deep within him. Without being bored, free from all desire, unaware of the passage of time, prepared to remain indefinitely immersed in the solitary OM, but equally prepared, if the Spirit so guides, even to take up again conversation with men. For the OM is complete sufficiency and complete fullness.

The nothingness is not exclusion, but fullness indeed. The nothingness into which the experience of Transcendence plunges one is none other than the fullness of the experience of Immanence. He who considers being surrounded by people or being apart from people as two separate experiences has not begun to understand what true aloneness is.

The monk is the man of the *eschaton*. It is he who, through whatever religious expression Providence had called him to, bears witness to the fact that God is beyond all things. It is he who bears witness to the fact that time has come from eternity and is returning to eternity. He is the witness of *advaita,* of the non-duality of being through all the changing seasons and multiplicity of material forms. He it is who reminds men by his solitude and by his very freedom that no word can possibly express who God is, nor any praise be worthy of him. Whatever he is, the role of the *sannyasi* is that of the spirit; he passes beyond and bursts open all manifestations, *murtis,* expressions of the divine which are essentially relative. As the Spirit, in the Spirit, he is in some sense the return of everything to the Father, to the Source, to the Silence which preceded all things, to the one and only OM.... — *Mountain,* 166–77

## THE ROLE OF CONTEMPLATIVES

In the last few weeks I have been thinking that solitude — complete solitude — is marvelous, and in the end easy, provided only that one does not try to compensate for the absence of human society by substitutes (either actual or wished for, and on excellent pretexts): receiving or making visits, study, reading, writing.... All these are good; but in the case of a contemplative they are only a relief for his weakness. He has a different part to play. His part is not to have a part, and his function not to have a function. In the world he is a witness to God, to that in God which cannot be expressed or manifested, to God insofar as he is beyond reach, etc.; and before God he bears witness that man has accepted that God should truly be the beyond. That he should "remain there" is enough for God; and anyone for whom that is not enough has understood nothing of his "call" to solitude. If God wishes to use him in the world of men, it is for God to make him understand this; so long as the "inspiration" to act, write, study, make foundations, is not clear, the solitary ought not to stir from his place.

—FT, December 29, 1959, *LS&T,* 131

## SOLITUDE AND EMPTYING

The life of solitude *at the outset* normally calls for rather strict use of time and for some work that is reasonably absorbing. My own experience of this is supported by that of others; but I think one has to get free from this as soon as possible. It seems to me that the hermit should normally be free and available for prayer at all times, and that it should probably be sufficient for him to ward off the temptation to sloth, if he always has at hand some serious work, I mean some solid reading that requires concentration, which he can take up when he is not capable of keeping himself recollected. You know the old formula of "lectio divina," handed down especially in the Benedictine tradition. That is what should be the normal occupation of the hermit. So much then as regards a life of enduring solitude.

As regards a retreat? A retreat is not a time *for getting information about* God by reading, or for *giving him information* in prayers made up of petitions, thanksgiving etc. (I got these expressions from an English Quaker friend, who seems to have hit the nail on the head); at least this applies to the retreat of contemplatives. A retreat is for listening to him, being recollected in his presence, forgetting oneself, allowing him to be in oneself, soaking oneself in his real nature (Tauler's superessence), in fact, to use a favorite expression of mine, it is a time simply to *be*. When I said this to a Kashmiri who came to Shantivanam about two years ago, he looked at me with some amazement, and then a few days later told me his wonder at "simply being." As for a Christian, this simple word (namely, "I am") has overtones that are even deeper and more wonderful than for a Hindu.

Three years ago I spent five weeks in total solitude in a closed room, being given my food through a hatch. It was built for this special purpose by some Hindu friends who spent periods in it every year (one of them stays there for three or four months without a break). The only books that I took with me were a Latin N.T. and some extracts from the Upanishads. I read them very sparingly, and chiefly used them to remind myself of the most significant texts. If one totally accepts, grasps, and clings to this solitude, this silence from reading books, this quieting even of interior speculation, and does so with one's whole heart, without reserve, without seeking to make for oneself substitutes, then I believe that in a soul that is already interiorized, the "lotus" cannot fail to open. More and more, as the days pass, everything seems far, far away, and only what is essential abides. Nothing is either heard or seen (I refer to inner experience), for it is precisely there that the danger would lurk for souls with a psychic weakness. But the emptying will take place.

—FT, March 3, 1960, *LS&T*, 131–32

## THE GREAT SOLITUDE
## WITHIN THE SOUL

I am very rushed this morning, but even so I must certainly arrive in time to sing the Alleluia with you.... Everything external, the liturgical life itself, is all beautiful. But there is something more beautiful still, namely, what is "within," where beyond all imagining we discover the God of whom there is neither image not idea...the great solitude within the soul, to which India constantly calls us back; for, as I have already said, it is here that I have at last learned to be a monk.

—MT, April 1, 1955, *LS&T,* 127

*In an essay called simply "Esseulement"(solitude) — Abhishiktananda wrote at length about a solitude that is sometimes unbearable.*

## FROM "ESSEULEMENT"

This state originates in [anyone who commits himself for good to the way of knowledge] discriminating between what is real and what is transitory, *viveka,* which more and more impresses itself on his mind under the influence of his faith in the scriptures and his master, and also of his own reflection guided by teaching and the sacred texts. The fact is that the way of *gnosis* is not simply the intellectual pursuit which too frequently has characterized philosophical research in the West and likewise has often marked theological speculation. The discovery of the Real involves the whole being.

But the cause of this solitude is to be sought, far more than in faith and thought, in the increasingly marked influence on his attitude of a kind of warmth or inner light. One might say that it is the influence of that original condition that is his own, the natural, innate, or *sahaja* condition, beyond his own consciousness, or rather at the subtle center of his mental core. His reflections on his faith and on the essentially contingent value of everything that is not the Absolute are reinforced and immeasurably amplified by this "instinct," this sense, which then shows itself by its effects, no longer in himself: i.e. the sphere of the gifts of knowledge and understanding.

This produces, as of necessity, a more and more complete disenchantment with all that is not the Absolute and the Absolute in itself. And this disenchantment cannot fail to impinge on matters of religion. Their relativity as regards time, space, human beings, etc., appears in such a bright light that the intelligence, athirst for absolute truth, can no longer find satisfaction in them, nor can desire, athirst for absolute good, take any pleasure in them. The most essential elements of the faith lose the *flavor* of truth. Even the doctrines of the Trinity and the Incarnation can no longer speak to the soul. The soul is absolutely compelled to lose the Triune God and the God-Man as it has conceived them, and to allow itself to be swallowed up in the abyss of Being, of the Godhead beyond all conceiving, which attracts it irresistibly. For it there is no question of wanting or not wanting this; it has no choice in the matter. This loss is unavoidable, whether or not it is pleasing to the soul. It is totally impossible for him to hold on to the elements of the magnificent synthesis in which he had hitherto delighted, or which people now suggest to him from outside. And no more is it a help to hear himself condemned for pride and unbelief — rather the opposite, it plunges him even deeper into this terrible isolation.

Nothing then remains for him but naked faith, that is to say, faith reduced to a nucleus which is so essential that the intelligence no longer has any purchase on it....

Neither does creation reveal to the soul the fullness of the Father, nor does the Incarnation that of the eternal and consubstantial Son, nor does the church with its saints and prophets enable the soul to penetrate to the ultimate depths of the Spirit. In the very fact that they lead the soul towards being in itself, they seem to cry out to it from the greatest depth of their mystery: Go beyond, do not halt anywhere! Go to the Father in himself, to that in him which is and always will be beyond all manifestation. Go to the Son in himself, to that in him which is beyond every formulation of the Word, of the Utterance which he is. Go to the Spirit, and be lost in this absolute End, which springs from the opening up of the Godhead in the essential Begetting, and fulfils it in the non-duality which it is, both personal and final. Thus the human words in which Revelation is expressed now lose in the slight of the soul all value and all taste of eternity and absoluteness. Only the Eternal in Itself and only the Absolute in Itself could satisfy it, and neither the Eternal nor the Absolute in itself is within the range of human thought.

At this moment the most beautiful arguments concerning creation which might be proposed to him are incapable of touching him. He has deep in himself something which he cannot explain — a taste not consciously savored, a sense beyond all feeling of the Absolute which prevents him from feeling any quality of being in creation inasmuch as it is created. He can only whisper with the ancient Sages: *ekam eva advitiyam,* one, alone, and non-dual. Of the creation he can neither say that it is, since God alone IS, nor can he say that it is not; he is involved with a world which his eyes see, which his ears hear, and which his hands touch. He is urged to take up a position, to declare whether this world of manifestation, of *maya,* is real for him, or not. What answer could he honestly give, what meaning could these questions really have for him? *Maya,* the world, is for him something irrational. He will not be happy to use that big word "cosmic illusion," for that still has to be decided; and who is he to make such a decision concerning reality?

All that he knows is that Being is and alone is, and that if anything has being, it is only through and in the One who alone IS; and yet there is nothing apart from being (*asparsa*) and there is nothing within being (*akhanda*). For him this is the unfathomable mystery which no philosophy can explain, on the brink of the abyss to which every true philosophy can only lead, since reasoning is incapable of encompassing being....

Herein is the paradox of society: the individual emits society, and society helps the individual; and yet my brother — however loving and devoted he may be — cannot eat for me, nor can he attain the Absolute on my behalf. I alone can attain my end. In this situation all help is a useless burden; every attempt to help me only has the result of thrusting me deeper into the abyss of my solitude by making me realize that in the end I depend entirely on myself. And this I myself, what is it? I cannot even find myself any longer. Nothing to lean on, beside me, behind me, before me, above or below me. My brothers no doubt seek to help me, but each one invites me to take a different path; and all their paths seem in my view to revolve within the narrow circle to which the world is reduced, whereas what I really need is a sure way of leaping outside this circle, or else I need to find this circle beyond that circle in which the experience of the Absolute has set me. The agony itself is from this world that passes away and yet claims to be comparable to eternity.

It is agonizing that everyone cries out to me that I must at all costs recover my footing for fear of being lost, whereas I no longer have any real desire for myself. The church is divine, and the Spirit guides it; however what a terrible *kenosis* of the Spirit there is in the church! As seen by history and from a phenomenological point of view everything in its development is quite simply explained by sociological laws. So where is one to go? And as the call of the Absolute becomes more pressing, so the church's warning is more and more seriously and poignantly repeated.

And the more the church cries out that I should cling to her, the only fortress of eternal life, so even more powerfully the cry comes to me from the greatest depth of my experience of being: What then is there that is impermanent, what is there that passes away, that might be capable of attaining the permanent, of coming to that which does not pass away? Nothing could attain to being if it was not being already; nothing would pass into eternity if its dwelling, its origin, its place of springing up was not already eternity. Simply realize, O man, what you are!

"I looked but there was no one to help" (Isaiah 63:5).

— *Intériorité et révélation: Essais théologiques*

## THE CALL OF THE WITHIN

From the moment she turns her gaze inward, the soul encounters the *sign* of the God within, his image, his "angel," as the Old Testament would say. Soon she experiences an ineffable joy in the company of the beloved Host, within the bosom of the Three, as she worships, gives thanks, surrenders herself in self-offering, repentance and expiation, intercedes.... Moreover the soul senses in the here and now, as being already fulfilled for herself, the promises of Jesus according to St. John:

> "My Father will love him and we shall come and make our abode in him...."

For the Hindu this is the stage of *saguna Brahman,* of God "with form," of intense spiritual devotion, *bhakti,* of the "games" of Shiva who reveals himself in love to his devotees or those of the gopis and the divine Gopala or Herdsman, of souls and their divine Lover.

Then comes the moment when the Host within, reaching deeper and deeper, draws the soul herself to more and more profound levels of her own inner being. There is a penetration of the self, which little by little, seems to become a breathtaking descent into a void, an engulfing in an abyss. The soul loses her foothold... in a way that may well resemble what happens at the moment of death, when the soul experiences the withdrawal from her of her bodily senses — while at the same time she herself seems to withdraw from them — and every contact with the world that they used to signify and every involvement of herself in the world that they used to indicate and every penetration of that same world into herself that they used to facilitate; very soon she feels also the withdrawal of conscious thought, of the will, of all that inner world with which the soul had gradually become identified.... Till it is as if the soul, the self, had no longer any support. It is an engulfing, as it were, into a Self which is so profound, so all-embracing and yet at the same time so simple, so non-complex, that Self which is so essential, so primordial, that the soul has no longer anything to grasp, nowhere to lodge. She feels herself swept away into a "beyond" that is yet part of her very own being, where even her awareness of separate existence altogether disappears.

This is the unique experience of *kevala,* of the Absolute, of Alone-ness, the experience of the infinite Alone-ness of God; not of alone-ness with God, nor alone-ness in God, but of the Alone infinitely and essentially Alone, the alone-ness that is the Alone-ness of God. It is the experience of *ekam eva advitiyam,* of the One alone and without a second, of the One for whom there is no other, of the one-ness in which there is no longer room for "knower" and "known," for lover and beloved.... That "night" of which St. John of the Cross spoke, a night of bliss and also of anguish: "In dark night, from my habitation where all was peace, I stole away without being seen."

— *Guhantara,* chapter 3, MR Coll.

# 6

# Christianity

ॐ

*Is it possible to be drawn irresistibly to Hindu advaita and to remain a Christian? This is the question at the heart of Abhishiktananda's long and anguished struggle, and in the course of it he thought and wrote deeply on what it means to be a Christian. He had a great need to work out these issues, often writing without any view to publication. One such article was a long piece entitled "What Is a Christian?" Here is part of it.*

## WHAT IS A CHRISTIAN?

There is but one Reality and one alone, the community of life which exists at the heart of Being, between the Father and the Son, in the unity of the Spirit. That alone is; and it is within this community of life that the man who is has his existence.

Man seems to have lost the wonderful meaning of this little word "is," the simplest and most common in his language. Yet it is the name which God disclosed as being his very own, when Moses questioned him on Mount Horeb. "I am who I AM," said God. Then Moses descended from the mountain and said to the people: "I AM is sending me to you" (Exod. 3:13).

Some centuries later when the Jews were disputing with Jesus in the Temple at Jerusalem, Jesus said to them: "When you have lifted up the Son of man, then you will know that I AM" (John 8:28).

When in her search for God the soul penetrates deeper and deeper, from abyss to abyss — or, if we prefer, climbs higher and higher from peak to peak — being increasingly dissatisfied with what created beings tell her of God or with what her own thoughts enable her to glimpse, urged on from within by the Spirit who will not let her halt at any sign but pushes her inexorably towards that which is beyond sign, towards that which finally no sign can ever represent or reveal — then, at the last, when she is utterly incapable of saying that God is this or that, like this or like that (for all concepts are powerless to encompass him, all descriptions impotent to qualify him) the last word that she attempts still to stammer before she relapses into utter silence is HE IS.

> No word, no thought can ever grasp him,
> No eye behold him.
> What way remains to reach him, save
> To say He IS. (*Katha Upanishad* 6.12)

Afterwards, if the soul who has experienced in this way the fiery intensity of Being returns to the world of things, Being shines for her there with such brilliance that she is henceforth incapable of seeing within them anything at all except HE who IS. No longer does she perceive a sign or a reflection, for her eye is fixed upon Being alone. Who can discern the splendor of the moon and the stars at the end of a clear night, however brightly they may shine, when once the sun has risen in the sky? Created beings, including the awareness of man, are only signs and reflections, material things without reason. Their reality consists only in manifesting in their beings and hymning the glory of the One who reveals himself in them. There is nothing in all the world, however deeply and secretly hidden in the heart of beings or, contrariwise, however superficial and ephemeral, that eludes the shining Presence of the One who discloses himself everywhere. There is nothing in all the world which is not full of the mystery of that-to-which-all-signs-point and which does not itself adumbrate that which goes beyond all signs. Fascinated by this Presence the soul who lives by faith no longer perceives anything at all except the One Who Is, Being-in-itself.

If at length the soul returns to herself and seeks to reach within herself,... then the further she goes the more deeply and ever more deeply opens before her the abyss. She looks for at least some little ledge where she may pause, take hold, recover breath. Irresistibly, inexorably, the gulf draws her; she reels, loses her foothold, is engulfed, loses herself. She strives to find a little nook from which she may just contemplate this Presence, just space enough to kneel, prostrate herself, worship, be it only for a moment... and there is nothing in her that is not already full of this Presence, for "Before Abraham was, I AM" (John 8:58); there is in her no place left, no spot in which she may declare "I, Me." Before ever this "I" is evidenced within her the abyss is already resounding with the *I* which God utters to himself from all eternity. There remains only a Presence, not a presence that has "come to be" but that which has always been, that in which all things are.

Is there not inherent in every presence a certain reciprocity? This presence at the heart of all is a presence of whom? to whom? between whom? By thrusting forward in search of this Presence the soul loses herself. One cannot see God and live, as the scriptures say (Exod. 33:20). In Being only the Presence of God exists, in his mystery ineffable.

The Christian is the man who has accepted from Jesus this amazing revelation that he is because, by reason of his faith in the only Son of God, he too is a son.

The Christian knows, of course, very well that he is still "en route," a pilgrim, involved in becoming and in the flux of things; and this is the paradox of the Christian life. Yet he knows also that in his baptism he died, rose again and ascended to the heavens where he was placed with Jesus, for "faith can guarantee the blessings that we hope for, prove the existence of the realities that at present remain unseen" (Heb. 11:1). He possesses the pledge of the Spirit (Eph. 1:14), and the spirit within him, in the depths of his heart, bears witness that he is a child of God, gently and ineffably murmuring: Abba, Father (Rom. 8:15–16).

The Christian is not one who primarily busies himself with doing. He is primarily one who is intent upon the mystery of his existence, who in the depths of his heart humbly and simply accepts the fact that he is, in virtue of both his creation and his redemption. He has no other raison d'être in this world than to receive and transmit to all his powers of body and soul and extend through them to the whole world the radiance of this glorious awakening-to-being in the depths of the self in the blessed place of resurrection. The glory for which, in the night before his death, Jesus prayed to the Father must be extended to his whole Mystical Body and to the whole universe — the new heavens and the new earth of the Apocalypse. This is the task by whose progress time is measured and which reaches its fulfillment beyond time. It is a work of both Spirit and man in indissoluble partnership: there is an eternal summons to the Son proceeding from the Father and a constitutive reaching-out of the Son towards the Father — from which proceeds the one Spirit, the "breath of the Breath."

The Christian's true part, both by birth and by right of sonship, is, like that of Mary of Bethany, to remain silent and intent in the Presence of the Father; not, however, in the same way as one man can be in the presence of another, whether seen or in the imagination, but rather by a penetration of that Presence, which is the Presence of the Father to the Son and of the Son to the Father. At the very heart of this glory and this joy he listens to the Thou of Love addressed to him from all eternity by

God and he no longer has any right to utter his own I except from within the eternal I of the Father in the place where Being awakens to the Self. He then finds in the words of the Gospel a wonderful savor of life eternal, especially in those words which Jesus addresses to the Father and those in which he expounds to his disciples the secret of his life with the Father. The believer now hears these same words in his innermost self springing up as if from their very source, for in very truth the bosom of the Father from which Jesus utters them is the deepest place of his very own heart.

—Date unknown, believed to be unpublished,
trans. Mary Rogers, MR Coll.

*In the 1970s, when* Sagesse hindoue mystique chrétienne, *which had been first published in 1965, was being prepared for publication in English, Abhishiktananda wanted to rewrite it, as he was no longer satisfied with it, especially with the passages on the "theology of fulfillment." As it was he had to be content with renaming the book* Saccidananda — A Christian Approach to Advaitic Experience, *and with making a few changes. He did not feel these changes completely eradicated all traces of Christian triumphalism and was still not entirely happy with it — in fact he was working on the proofs until the day before his final heart attack. Nevertheless even in its original version the book brought encouraging responses from people who found it helped them to understand things that had happened to them in their own spiritual lives, for instance, recognizing their own experience in Abhishiktananda's experience of the Self, which he describes in the first chapters. One writer said that even John of the Cross had not been able to explain so clearly what he calls the "interior stripping" and "the passage from the 'self' to the 'Self.'" After its publication he received many letters that said, in effect, "Your book has taught me nothing new, but for the first time in my life I have understood what was happening in my soul."* This convinced Abhishiktananda that he was *"not heading in the wrong direction."* Today, thirty-five years later, more and more people are having these experiences and Abhishiktananda becomes more and more relevant. All the passages quoted in this book are from the revised English version of Saccidananda.

## IS IT POSSIBLE TO LIVE ACCORDING TO THE GOSPEL?

Is it possible to live quite literally according to the Gospel? A very few individuals like Francis of Assisi have indeed taken it completely seriously, but as a rule its paradoxes have been frozen into formulas and institutions in order to comply with the dictates of "common sense."

In fact the Gospel is a direct challenge to that so-called common sense. It says: The present moment is all that matters; tomorrow is God's business. Sell all that you have and give the proceeds to the poor, to those who are unable to make you any return. Do not store up anything for tomorrow, any more than do the birds of the air. Leave behind your fields, your wife and children, your father and mother, and come with me; follow me, carrying the cross on your shoulder like a criminal on the way to his execution. If anyone asks you for anything, give it at once. It anyone wants to slap your face, offer him your cheek. Never oppose force with force. You are indeed fortunate if you have nothing, if you are sad, if you are hungry and thirsty. You are even more fortunate if people insult you, persecute you, put you to death....

The life of one who literally obeys the Gospel is that of a stranger, a homeless wanderer, one who goes from place to place, never settling anywhere for good, but always about to set off again. Wherever he goes he does good to all just as his master did, even to those who curse him; and to all who are ready to listen he passes on the message of love and the news of the Kingdom. He asks for nothing, but accepts everything, insults and injuries included, calmly and peacefully. He does not worry about anything and is not attached to anything, but always and everywhere he radiates the joy and peace with which his soul overflows. Such were in fact the standing orders which Jesus himself gave to his Apostles, when he sent them out in advance to announce the Kingdom.

The wandering Indian *sannyasi* is indeed very similar to the itinerant messenger of the Gospel. Like him he is free from all anxiety or preoccupation, being without attachment of any kind, whether to things, places, or people. Wherever he goes he is a stranger, and yet everywhere he finds himself at home.... The alms he receives from house to house are sufficient for his daily food, and a rag picked up by the roadside is good enough for a loincloth; at midday the shade of a tree protects him from the hot sun, and at night the projecting eaves of any building can serve as his shelter.

Just as Francis of Assisi took his Christian calling seriously and did not try to "interpret" the Gospel, so the Indian ascetic takes equally seriously his own calling to be in truth a knower of brahman, *brahmavid, atmavid.* For he knows well that it is only by fleeing far away from everything, and in the first place from himself, by passing beyond everything, and above all beyond himself, that man can attain to God, the Unattainable. How could a "seer" like this conceivably take seriously the Gospel message, when the preacher himself has not yet taken his Christian calling with equal seriousness? Only one who has been reborn in the Spirit and has allowed himself in the same Spirit to sound the very depths of God can bear witness to the mystery of the Father and the Son, and can pass on the consuming fire of the Christian message, which speaks at once of God's inaccessibility and of his nearness. — *Saccidananda,* 8–10

## "MY FATHER AND I ARE ONE"

Jesus himself does not seem ever to have felt any of the anguish that mystics of every tradition so often feel when confronted with the infinity of God. He never felt that the *You* which he addressed to the Father separated him in any way from God. To be from God and to be one with God, in the depths of Jesus' consciousness these were essentially and quite naturally one. They were not successive moments in an experience which could be measured in length of time, nor did they indicate the different levels at which a unique experience would manifest itself in differing ways. Rather it was a case of non-duality — in the proper sense of the word — between his experience of oneness with, and his experience of otherness from, God his Father. That reason should balk at this is not surprising. Nevertheless Jesus' testimony still stands and cannot be evaded.

The experience of the Absolute to which India's mystical tradition bears such powerful witness is all included in Jesus' words: "My Father and I are one." All that the Maharshi, and countless others before him, knew and handed on of the inexorable experience of non-duality, Jesus also knew himself, and that in a preeminent manner. We need only refer to his words. "He who has seen me has seen the Father" (John 14:9). Whatever the Father does, he does through the Son; whatever the Son does, it is the Father doing it through him. And yet, at the very heart of all this, there remains the "face-to-face" of the Son and the Father.

The conclusion is inescapable: the experience of Jesus includes the advaitic experience, but it certainly cannot be reduced to the commonly accepted formulation of that experience. Vedanta obliges us to recognize in man a level of consciousness deeper than that of reflective thought, more basic than man's awakening to himself through sense-perception or mental activity. Christ's experience compels us to admit the existence in man of something even deeper still.... If, as non-Christians maintain, Jesus is only a man, then whatever natural endowments he possesses must necessarily be available to every man. And if he is the Son of God, as Christians believe, then they must not forget that, according to their faith, Jesus shares with them by grace all that he possesses by right of his divine Sonship. —*Saccidananda*, 82–83

*Whatever his problems with the church, Abhishiktananda never wavered in his devotion to Jesus. Jesus for whom the heavens opened, Jesus his true guru, Jesus in the mystery of* advaita, *Jesus in the cave of the heart.*

## JESUS

Jesus showed himself in human form at Easter for those who could not accept otherwise that he was alive. At Pentecost he expressed himself through the gifts of the Spirit to those to whom he had given the responsibility of spreading the Word. But the privileged, those who he had chosen simply to say with him I AM within the heart of the Father, beyond all human form and all manifestation of the Spirit, he takes them with him to his ascension, beyond all heavenly worlds, also beyond all sight, all thought, even there, where there is nothing but the silence of the last sound of Om. OM. OM. OM. OM. OM. The heart says it at each beat, about each second breath. OM. OM. OM. OM. OM. The passing on of OM is precisely one of the essential points of the *diksha* (initiation) of *sannyasa*. With the great words (*mahāvākya*) the guru says "Tat, tvam, asi: Thou are that" and the disciple replies: "Aham Brahma asmi: I am Brahman." At the baptism of Jesus, the heavens opened and from the cave came the word, My Son.

—MT, July 1973, KA

## JESUS, THE TRUE GURU

The little cave, the place of peace and joy, is an enclosure far stricter than that of a monastery. The grilles that guard it are grilles of love. No one ever enters there except Jesus and the soul. Rather, there is no one there but Jesus, and only the soul has the right to enter it. Others may indeed open the door and at first show the way, and even push you inside — that is the role of the guru. But once you have entered, then it is the true guru that shows himself, the master of truth, Jesus. He speaks without the sound of words, and we know then that in all the circumstances of life he is speaking words of love that he alone can utter; and that is all he says, and all he does are caresses, even if at times his hand feels heavy. This cave we call in Sanskrit *guha*. Long ago it was discovered by the *rishis* of the Vedas. There indeed it was that the Blessed Virgin shut herself away to think of Jesus.... See in the Gospel... "Mary kept all these things in her heart."

—MT, February 2, 1957, *LS&T*, 127

## JESUS IN *ADVAITA*

Jesus is this mystery of *advaita* in which I can no longer recognize myself *separately*. Lost as much in the space of the heart as in that of the span of the universe, as much in the Source as in the shining, the radiance that empties me. And I am Fullness, *purnam*, precisely in this letting-go of myself everywhere. ... And my *purnam* is precisely this emptiness of all self.

—December 14, 1971, *Diary*, 336–37, quoted in SETU, no. 20

## FOR ASCENSION DAY

When we love in pure faith we feel nothing, and that is all to the good; for as long as we feel that we love him, we are not loving him in earnest, because basically what we are loving is not him, but the pleasure we take in loving him. So long as we *taste* peace, whether inwardly or outwardly, it is not *his* peace, because his peace "passes all understanding," as St. Paul says. It is not our own joy that is our goal, but, as the Lord says in the Gospel to the good and faithful servant: "Enter into the joy of your Lord." It is his own joy that is our goal, not yours, and so anything you feel is like having the scent of something far away — it is of no interest. What matters is his own joy, which draws me without my being aware of it, his own peace likewise. Whatever may take place outside the body or in the body, or even in the mind itself, has nothing to do with the Jesus in the joy of his Father's bosom, which is "the joy of the Lord," and which is in the deepest center of our heart. All the things that happen to me, what do they matter?...The truth is there, beyond all that we can feel or touch.... So, when one knows that, death has no further importance. Concern about one's death, whether in fear or from desire, is quite simply egotistical, a return on the self. Death is his business, not mine. What about the importance of the moment of death? But every moment is just as important as that of my death — the moment when I drink my soup or wash my feet, just as much as when I pray or nestle close to the Lord. For it is at every moment of my life, even the most commonplace, that I enter into the joy of the Lord, which is the eternal Son. I also am begotten as the child of the heavenly Father in his heart of love. Death after a quarter of an hour, death after eighty years! Once I have come to dwell in the Father's heart, in the depth of the cave, that is to say, in eternity, what can *time* possibly have to do with me there?...

At the Ascension Jesus came to the bosom of the Father, and we neither see nor hear him any more. Heaven is not the stratosphere or the place of sputniks; it is the deepest center of my heart, so deep that even my thought cannot reach it. I know he is there, and that is all. —MT, May 9, 1958, *LS&T*, 128–29

## CHRIST AND THE CHURCH

Dr. Mehta and others want to have me make a distinction between Christ and the church. The Christ whom I find in my ultimate depth is as far from the Christianity that men have made as is the *kevala* from the God of their thoughts!

The Spirit beyond the church, the Father beyond the Son. The Christ beyond the church and beyond the Christ of history is still more really the Christ, the living God!

Beyond the Christ there is always Christ. Beginning from the man born of Mary. Christ is the mystery of *sat*.

—April 1, 1957, *Diary*, 202

## *SACCIDANANDA* — A DEFINITION

Saccidananda *is one of the deepest Hindu insights concerning God and has trinitarian overtones beloved by Abhishiktananda. It is a combination of three Sanskrit words* Sat *(Being),* Cit *(awareness),* ananda *(bliss).*

*Sat* (Being). In my own depth, beyond all perceiving, all thought, all consciousness of distinction, there is the fundamental intuition of my being, which is so pure that it cannot be adequately described. It is precisely here that I meet God, in the mystery at once of my own being and of his. This in fact is the *sat* on which the Upanishadic seers made their meditations. In the last resort, what can I say of myself except that "I am," as we are powerfully reminded by the experience which came to Ramana Maharshi as a youth? Just so, all that I can truly say of God is simply that "He is." This is what was revealed to Moses at Horeb, and it was also realized intuitively by the *rishis:*

> It is only by saying "He is"
> that one may reach him!
> —*Katha Upanishad*, 6, 12

"He is" — nothing more can be said of him. He simply is, because he is. When my consciousness is pure enough to give a perfect reflection, then pure being, *sat*, mysteriously and inexorably reveals itself in me in its utter simplicity; indeed, it not merely discloses itself to me, but it also takes me up into its own simplicity and absoluteness. It makes me realize that my very being and existence is nothing other than its own being and existence. And yet this *sat*, for all that it is the deepest reality of every creature, remains infinitely beyond any of them. Nothing can hold it. It is forever beyond the reach of any attempt to define it, or to think or speak of it. In its very immanence it is infinitely transcendent.

*Sat* is also *satyam*, truth, because being and the true are identical. Truth is the unveiling of Being, of the Real, both in itself and in me. It is in the *sat* that I myself also am real and true, real with its reality and true with its truth, for what can subsist apart from it? No truth or reality can be outside it.

*Cit* (Awareness). I am, and I can know that I am. This is the whole mystery of the human consciousness, the *cit* of Hindu tradition. Indeed, from the beginning nature contained within itself the potentiality of this self-awareness, which acted as a hidden force in promoting the development of the cosmic process. Finally in man the universe attained to self-awareness, the presence of the self to itself, in which alone *sat* becomes luminous and resplendent (if one may put it so) within itself....

*Ananda* (Bliss). For St. Gregory of Nyssa the yardstick of man's blessedness is the extent of his resemblance to God. Bliss is to gain access to the Original through beholding the image in the mirror of a pure heart.

So also for India's seers, bliss is to arrive at the final secret of the self, at the very point where man returns again to his Source and there discovers his own ultimate truth. When indeed pure self-awareness has been sufficiently realized, it is as if the whole being were flooded with an inexpressible sense of completion, peace, joy, and fullness, the *ananda* of Hindu tradition. Every desire and every need find their satisfaction — indeed, they are both fulfilled and transcended. At that point, a man forgets his existential anguish, his terror of not-being, the source of all his anxiety and fears. All inner disharmony is quieted in the transcendent unity of being and of being aware of being....

*Tat tvam asi* ('You are That"). In my own innermost center, in the most secret mirror of my heart, I tried to discover the image of him whose I am, of him who lives and reigns in the infinite space of my heart. But the reflected image gradually grew faint, and soon it was swallowed up in the radiance of its Original. Step by step I descended into what seemed to me to be successive depths of my true self — my being, my awareness of being, and my joy in being. Finally nothing was left but he himself, the Only One, infinitely alone, Being, Awareness, and Bliss, *Saccidananda*. In the heart of *Saccidananda* I had returned to my Source.

*Tat tvam asi,* "You are That!" were the last words I heard before I fell asleep in the slumber of Being, before I "laid me down and slept..." (Ps. 3:5).

> He gazed at the image in himself;
> but the image vanished in the Self;
> nothing remained of my gazing
> only That which was gazed at....
> — *Saccidananda,* 167–72

## THE TRINITY

If the Christian experience of the Trinity opens up to man new vistas of meaning in the intuition of *Saccidananda,* it is equally true that the terms *sat, cit,* and *ananda* in their turn greatly assist the Christian in his own meditation on that central mystery of his faith. No single theological language will ever be able to express all that the Gospel has revealed to us concerning God who is Father, Son, and Holy Spirit. It is therefore to be expected that, just as Judaism and Hellenism have made their contributions, so the divine preparation of India in its turn will serve to lead believers to contemplate the mystery in a new depth. In particular, the intuition of *Saccidananda* will be an aid in penetrating the mystery of the Spirit which, according to St. John's Gospel, relates chiefly to God's presence to men in their hearts. And if anyone comes to the Gospel with personal experience of Vedanta, it can be said with assurance that the Gospel words will elicit profound echoes from the intuition which he had already had of *Saccidananda;* and that in turn this previous experience will cause marvelous harmonics to sound in his present faith in the Holy Trinity. This is because all things are the work of the one Spirit, who has been preparing for this man's awakening and resurrection, ever since long ago he first revealed himself to the heart of the *rishis* as the infinite Presence.
—*Saccidananda,* 177–78

## THE TWO EXPERIENCES OF THE TRINITY AND OF *SACCIDANANDA*

The Christian cannot but rejoice and give thanks to the Lord that the Vedantic experience of the Self leads on to the trinitarian experience of *Saccidananda.* But at the same time he cannot overlook the fact that his conviction of this depends on faith alone.

How can the Christian mystic possibly prove that his trinitarian experience of *Saccidananda* really does go beyond and transcend the experience of the Hindu *jnani*? Once the sphere of Being, of the Self, has been reached, all the categories with which so far the intellect has operated are thrown into confusion — that is, the notions before and after, here and beyond, inside and outside, all that is comprehended under the form of *dvandva*, the pairs of opposites. Everywhere he meets simply with *Being*, the indivisible and attributeless Brahman, as the sage puts it in the *Mundaka Upanishad* 2, 11:

> Brahman indeed is this — Immortality;
> Brahman before, Brahman behind;
> Brahman to the right, Brahman to the left;
> Brahman above, Brahman below;
> All this — Brahman!

Within this blinding intuition of Being, how can the Christian be sure that what he believes he has discovered about himself and the world in God through the biblical revelation of the Trinity is true? It seems rather that all this is merely a last-minute attempt to salvage what he cannot bear to abandon when he comes to make the final plunge into the abyss that attracts him so powerfully. The theme of a "communion of being" within the indivisible unity of being...at the heart of *advaita*, appears to be merely a supreme effort of the human intellect — at once sublime and desperate — to escape from the shipwreck that threatens it. The human mind would seem to be making a last attempt to save what it can of its experience of individuality and multiplicity by carrying back this experience into the depths of Being itself. Nothing but the magnificent trinitarian theology worked out by the early Fathers seems able to satisfy the human intellect and to rescue it from the despair that awaits it when it comes to peer into the abyss of Being. But in the last resort, what is this theology? Is it the supreme truth, or is it merely the intuition of some intellectual genius, elaborated by other great minds, which still must inevitably remain merely at the level of thought, of the *eidos?*

When Sri Ramana "returned" from his experiences — this "return" was only figurative, since in reality he never returned from it, nor does anyone who has truly had this experience — he looked in the world. Everywhere he saw nothing but the reality of Being, indivisible, limitless. Everywhere he heard the OM, the *aham*, the essential unique *I*. When the Christian mystic "returns" from his own experience, he perceives everywhere in the world the signs of the presence of the trinitarian mystery. In every rustling leaf, in every gentle breeze, in every moment and every event either in nature or history, he hears the *Thou* in which Being awakes to itself, he recognizes the *Abba Father* which the Spirit whispers in the hearts of God's elect.

— *Saccidananda*, 195–96

*For years Abhishiktananda went to Mass daily; it was almost compulsive. Then, much later, he went through a phase of not going to Mass; the compulsion was almost equally strong, for during the long periods when he was torn between Christianity and* advaita *the Mass was, as he said, "the crystallization of my inner drama." Eventually he reached the stage when he was free — free to go to Mass, free not to go to Mass. Then "Each Mass fulfils everything." This is Abhishiktananda's account of a Mass celebrated with a friend on the banks of the Ganges.*

## MASS

First of all, we threw off our clothes and plunged into the icy water. Thus in this predestined place we fulfilled the cosmic rite of returning to the original matrix, to the source of Being. It was also a reminder of the rite of Baptism, which gathers up and completes the cosmic rite symbolizing so powerfully the mystery of our regeneration.

Then, when the moment came, we settled down in our chosen spot surrounded by boulders. On the flat stone which we had managed to make sufficiently level, we spread out the fair linen, the Missal, and the silver chalice. We took a cup of water from the very source of the river. As bread for the offering and consecration we had brought with us one of the chapattis, unleavened bread, which is the ordinary food of the pilgrims. We tried in vain to light the candles, for the wind managed to extinguish them each time. However, sticks of incense took the place of candles for us. And there, high above at the zenith, was the great light of the firmament whose rays made the snows all around us a dazzling white: this same sun which sees all that takes place on the surface of the earth, which was reflected in the eyes of the first man, and which was seen by the eyes of Jesus as he was nailed to the cross; this sun, which is always present and witness of all that is, was, or will be, looked down upon us.

We sat cross-legged facing one another, and before beginning the liturgical celebration we first sang some special verses chosen from the Upanishads and then a Sanskrit litany in praise of the Savior, Son of God and Son of Man, the One Lord. Was our Eucharist not plunged deep into the cosmic rite, the Vedic rite as it was here?

The Eucharist continued slowly and discreetly to unfold. But it was in vain that we tried to raise our voices in order to hear one another give the responses; the voice of the river drowned all other sounds like the accompaniment of great organs. Was it not the mystery of the Voice of the Spirit which fills everything and in which all that is said of God and to God is caught up and given perfect expression? Together we sang the Our Father;

we exchanged the Kiss of Peace; we divided the bread; together we drank the sacred cup.

The sacrifice was consummated. On the banks of the Ganges, at its very source, the eschatological offering had been celebrated. In the sacrifice of the Lamb everything had finally been brought to completion; every prayer and chant that had been prayed or sung in these places, everything that had been offered symbolically in the temple or near the flowing water, all the trials and tribulations of the pilgrims, all the silence and the self-denial of the *munis,* everything had been finally gathered up.

From its Source the Ganges continued to descend towards the plains, first as a tumultuous torrent, and soon as a broad peaceful river bringing with it fertility and, in a mystic way, grace.

It was the Feast of the Sacred Heart, the Source.

— *Mountain,* 173–74

# 7

# God

ॐ

*Murray Rogers had a fond memory of Abhishiktananda once saying to him, in a hushed voice, "Murray, is there anything but God?" This way of thinking pervades everything Abhishiktananda said or wrote about God, for "God is beyond all notions. They are only spring-boards to be used for diving — and the spring-board is not the lake."*[1]

## THE EXISTENCE OF GOD

Although it might sound paradoxical, it would be true to say that it is not belief in the existence of God, the Absolute, for which faith is required. None can doubt the existence of *That Which Is* — even if precise formulations are quite another matter. Indeed the affirmation of God's existence is contained in the first *I* that is uttered by each awakening consciousness. But what really needs faith — and a faith that is particularly difficult for those who have been touched by the consuming fire of Being — is to believe in one's own existence in the presence of the Lord God, poor and feeble creature that one is by contrast with what is real and abiding. — *Saccidananda,* 115

---

1. OB, July 7, 1968, *LS&T,* 165.

## THE ESSENTIAL VOID

When man thinks seriously about God, striving to grasp him, to take his measure and mentally to realize his presence, his intelligence is soon baffled and reasoning plays him false. The time comes when thought itself vanishes in that overwhelming brightness. It is then as if the mind tries to escape from the unbearable presence of God, hunting desperately for itself apart from God, and seeking for survival in whatever form — something like the dove that Noah sent out from the Ark, which sought at least for a branch on which it could rest (Gen. 8:9). But all in vain. "Nature is then so denuded of form that it sinks into nothingness and is lost; all that remains is a simple IS and that IS is the One" (Eckhart, *Treatise* xi). Man is terrified of finding himself as "simply *being*." This appalls him more than anything. He believes that he cannot survive when God calls him to discover and contemplate himself in the mere act of existence, and he recoils from it. The absoluteness of being is as terrifying to him as non-being, since it as surely destroys all that he wants himself to be, or rather, wants to feel that he is.

Man would rather enjoy being something, no matter what, and prefers to live in his dreams, in the illusory image that he has constructed of himself, the world and God. However, if he is sincere, he soon wearies of his resistance to God and of his refusal to give himself up. God is stronger than he, and in his own time he lets this become apparent. When at length God draws a man into his own depths, all he can do is simply cry out in despair. Everything is torn away from him, alike in heaven and on earth, whether it belongs to the outer world or to the world within. He loses sight of every image of the Real which he had constructed for himself and in which he had planned to settle down — as if one could hope to settle anywhere in the world *of becoming*, which no doubt reveals being, but is powerless to comprehend it; or as if the form of this world was not passing away every moment (1 Cor. 7:31). There is nothing on which he can lay hold, to which he can cling. On the contrary, everything slips away — his body, his thought, his very awareness of himself and of his own personality. His being drawn within and called simply to *be* appears to him like being swallowed up in the void. Even in India many of those who received this call took fright at the supreme experience of depth; they strove to find some place to establish themselves, no matter how disagreeable or illusory it might be, and to hang there, poised between the world of reality, of being, and the world of *maya* or becoming. — *Saccidananda,* 104–5

## THE SECRET OF THE WITHIN

What is the within? What is the secret of the within? As you go deeper within yourself, the sheaths become more and more subtle which you weave around this within while you search for it, as if the within could be enclosed in anything. Is there a container of the void? Is there a cloak of *maya* for the Eternal? The within is only the within when you have not yet met it or found it.... The final prop on which you were relying in order to discover the supreme secret must be jettisoned in its turn. There is nothing, nothing any more, void, absolute *sunyata*. Even the idea of within vanishes when the within is attained....

There is no skin, no pulp, no kernel, no grain within the kernel, and no new elements within the grain. These are the successive layers of an onion, each one more flimsy; when you have removed the last one, nothing remains.... This nothing is the All.

OM TAT SAT. — December 6, 1953, *Diary,* 81, quoted in SETU, no. 21

## THE MEETING OF MAN WITH GOD

When, following the path traced by the ancient *rishis*, the Hindu sets out to discover the inner world beyond all sound and form, all word and thought — even beyond the necessary taste and experience of death and nothingness — there comes upon him finally the moment of complete renewal. This is a moment which is understood by the Christian in the context of the resurrection of the Lord after he had crossed beyond death and hell. The definitive meeting of man with God is birth beyond death. Man cannot see God without dying to self. No more can he attain himself in its supreme and definitive essence without dying and thus being born again — into the very sphere of God. Is it not this truth that the *Shivalinga* and the sanctuary which conceals it are seeking to express and symbolize in their own way? The dwelling of God on earth — which every temple symbolically aims to be — must necessarily be the place of man's renewal, a mysterious womb from which he springs forth anew, reborn in the deepest depths of the love of God as a beloved son chosen since the beginning of time, as the Christian says and knows, having been taught by the "inner unction" of the Spirit. — *Guru*, 60

## CONTEMPLATION OF THE TRANSCENDENT-IMMANENT GOD

The church's mission is as much in the desert as in the marketplace. In himself the Lord is everywhere. There is no being, no situation that cannot be the marvelous revelation of his Being. We fail to be recollected while working because we have constructed for ourselves an *idea* of God and imagine that we can find God only by means of this idea that we have made of him. So we have to think of him in one particular manner. And then, if we have to correct proofs or make the soup or drive a train, we are unable to bear in mind our idea of God. As if God was not just as much in the preparation of a tasty soup for his children or the careful handling of a railway train as he is in our beautiful meditations. This is precisely the lesson that the modern, materialistic, communist world has to teach...the lesson that God is giving us throughout this world. We have identified God, Christ, the church with the ideas that previous generations have formed of them. God is no longer the Transcendent One. But when God is truly realized as the Transcendent, his universal Immanence is simply overwhelming, for there is nothing that does not proclaim his presence. There is no man, no occupation, in which the eternal "My Son!" does not make itself heard. How can we be remote from him? The great silence itself in which God himself is, is not the negation of thoughts. It is its transcendence. It is compatible with every thought. God is not defiled by creating just as the lotus leaf holds water without becoming wet. What has creation added to God? What has the thought of the world added to his thought of himself? In thinking the world, he thinks himself, in loving his creatures, he loves himself. He never departs from himself. When you are using your typewriter you are entering the eternal act of exchange between the Father and the Son. Everything is a manifestation of Being, of the Supreme, the radiance of his Face which at once reveals and conceals him. I think I conveyed a little of this in the chapter "Ermites" on the subject of Work. We can only ever be distant from our conception of God, never from him. We can only ever be distant from our idea of ourselves, from the idea that we have constructed of our imagined perfection, never from ourselves in the truth of our being, which indeed is nothing else than our derivation from the source that has no sources....

And if we whose essential calling is to contemplation do not know this and do not tell it to others, then what use are we? A contemplative is not one who shuts himself away with the idea that he has formed of God and takes pleasure in it. The real contemplative is the man who has allowed the spirit of God to carry him off and to deprive him of every kind of prop, even in what he calls his contemplation. Totally bound and totally free. There is no conflict between this abiding in the Presence and paying attention to things. One should even say that there are two levels. For who can add anything whatever to God, and the son's act of gazing is a divine act. Do we add up essence and accidents? It is the All-ground that the soul perceives in everything when the Spirit is freely ruling in her. No duplication of the gaze. The Father knows nothing except in his Son, and the Son knows nothing except in his Father. He who has penetrated within knows that there is no within, and that it is merely called "within" in order to draw it out of its reality. The Father's heart is just a word, and all our words applied to God are to point out the path on which to let ourselves be carried away. So long as you cling to an idea of him, you do not have him. He has disappeared as soon as you think you have touched him. You possess him only when you have renounced his possession. When there is no one left to possess him, then he is possessed... for he alone possesses himself...

—TJ, January 1, 1962, *LS&T*, 144–45

## EVERYWHERE HE IS, AND ONLY HE

Man struggles hard to discover God and himself.
Too often, alas, he fails to find either God or himself.
He looks for God in some small corner of space.
But God fills the whole of space and transcends all space.
He looks for God at some point of time, in a past which
    once was, in a future which is still to come.

But God is outside all time. And eternity is present in each moment of *time*.

"The smallest abyss."
We must leap just the right distance, or else we shall miss our aim and find ourselves further off than ever, on a "further shore" which is not the true one.

God is too close to us. That is why we constantly fail to find him.
We turn God into an object — and God escapes our grasp.
We turn him into an idea — but ideas pass him by.
So Mary Magdalene was too much taken up with her thoughts about Jesus to be able to recognize him in the gardener at Calvary.

And Cleopas also was too caught up in his memories of Jesus to realize that it was he who was walking beside him on the way to Emmaus, until finally Jesus made himself known.
But, as he said to Thomas, blessed are those who recognize him at first sight!

Whoever has recognized him in his own self has recognized him in all.
Whoever has recognized him in the church, has recognized him in all that prepares the way for the church.
For the pure all things are pure.
And all things irresistibly recall the Spirit to one who has once been gently touched by the Spirit.
He should of course be aware of the different degrees of radiance which come from the transfigured Lord.

He knows that the perfect Light shone upon the earth only when He took flesh in whom at the beginning the Father said, *Fiat Lux,* Let there be Light!

And he also knows that the Spirit was given to mankind in his fullness only as the fruit of the Lord's resurrection.

However, seeing him everywhere in his signs, he cannot fail to recognize and adore him who is signified.
His faith makes up for the inadequacy of the signs.
Or rather, it is in his faith itself that the signs acquire their truth.
Whoever gazes at the midday sun can thereafter see nothing anywhere except the sun's blazing light.
Furthermore, all the colors are but the reflection of the sun.

Even blackness, the denial of light, is a sign of the sun, for without the sun and its light it could not even exist and none would be able to see it.
Everywhere the Lord extends his presence:
"From east to west he takes his course" (see Ps. 19:6).
Everywhere He is, and only He.
And yet, being in all things, he is distinct from all.

But the recognition that the Lord and his Spirit are everywhere present does not make any less urgent the task of announcing his resurrection and of declaring everywhere the message that "we have beheld his glory, glory as of the only Son from the Father, full of grace and truth!" (John 1:14).
Christ is the End of the Universe.
If we are required to work together with all our intelligence and physical strength for the progress of the world and the bodily and mental development of our fellowmen, we no less have the duty to take part, again with our whole strength and all the grace that we have received, in the fulfillment in Christ of this

world and in the ever more glorious advent of Christ in the heart and soul of every man.

No one has received anything except to share it with his brothers.

Even the church does not "possess" the Eucharist.

She is at the service of the Eucharist.

She offers it only so that, through the Eucharist, the world may pass from the sign that it is to the reality which it is called to be.

And the faithful only communicate as ministers to creation.

The Christian has therefore the duty to impart to his brother the Glory which he has received as a gift.

In him this Glory is filled with the promise of its manifestation.

It shines only in him to the extent that it radiates around him.

But for the Christian to be able to share his message with his brother — here his Hindu brother — and to impart to him this Glory, he must seek out and meet this brother at the place where he is, there where the Spirit has brought him and in him is waiting for the Christian

> at the heart of the cave of Arunachala,
> on the Further Shore of the self,
> at the Source!

Only there he will be able to make known to his brother that the very heart of Arunachala's cave is the Heart of Christ,

and that the Source is the Bosom of the Father, the Further Shore, where Jesus awaits him!

— Appendix, Two Poems, *Further Shore*, 120–22

## SEEK GOD

Seek God until you find him beyond all thought of him
  and all feeling of him —
beyond the thought you have of his being unthinkable,
beyond the feeling you have of his being impossible to
  experience.
And to seek God, seek also yourself,
beyond the subject of whom you are aware that he
  perceives, that he feels, that he thinks,
beyond the subject who is aware that he himself perceives
  himself, that he feels himself, that he thinks himself.
As long as you are still aware of yourself, you (yourself)
  will not have reached yourself.
You are as far from yourself as God is far from you,
God is as close to you as you are close to yourself,
God is as far from you within yourself as he is far from
  you outside yourself.
Scour the starry firmament, go beyond the galaxies, and
  you will not have reached God.
God's heaven is beyond all the heavens that beings can
  reach by their senses or their reason.
The mystery you bear within yourself is itself also beyond
  galaxies that your mind can explore.
God is as transcendent to you when you gaze at him
  within as when you gaze at him without.
And just as inaccessible.
And you yourself are as inaccessible to yourself as God
  within you is inaccessible to you.
For your own mystery is the very mystery of God.
And [it is] a mystery of God even deeper than the
  mystery of God in Himself — so the poor reason will
  stammer.

The divine immanence is at the furthest confines of the Transcendence.
And the immanent is in truth reached only at the heart of the transcendent. —June 14, 1956, *Diary,* 150

Can there be differences of degree in the presence of God?
—FT, July 7, 1960, *Life,* 145

# 8

# Prayer

ॐ

*Abhishiktananda's little book called simply* Prayer *is perhaps his most loved; certainly it is his most read. It was first published in 1967 and has since been reprinted many times.*

*Abhishiktananda was very practical about prayer, saying, for instance, that "there is as much true prayer when the whole attention is concentrated on an ache, as in the marvelous silence when we think we are in ecstasy."*[1]

*He was quite clear what he hoped the book would do: "May it awaken people to real prayer, that of silence in the heart, repeating the name of Jesus, or the Abba, or else the OM of the silence of the Spirit. Life is so good, despite everything, when you are awakened in the depth of the heart."*[2]

## GOD'S PRESENCE

Whether we like it or not, we are always present to God: it is utterly impossible not to be in his presence. There is no time and no place in our daily life, no occupation, however seemingly trivial, in which we are not before God. It is even wrong to say that there are times or occupations in which God is more

---

1. MT, September 2, 1972, *Life,* 310
2. MT, December 17, 1968, *Life,* 233–34.

present to us and we are more directly in touch with him. God in himself is essentially present to himself, always and invariably the same, the Eternal, the Infinite, the Almighty. He neither changes nor moves, neither comes nor goes. Always and everywhere he is himself, in his unique fullness. There is no sense, either symbolical or mythical, in which he can be more "here" or less "there," since he is indivisible.

In truth, it is to himself alone that God is present. From all eternity he is in himself and exists for himself. He enjoys forever the unspeakable bliss of his Presence to himself, the presence of the Father to the Son and of the Son to the Father, the even more mysterious presence of each to the Spirit and of the Spirit to each — that Spirit which is as it were the fruit of their mutual and undivided gaze of love.

The very reason for the coming on earth of Jesus the Son of God was to share with mankind that divine experience which was eternally his. He came to reveal to us what we are, each of us, in the personal call of the Father to each one of us. By means of his words which sprang out of his own experience — he himself being the eternal Word and the Expression of this essential experience within the very heart of God — he sought to awaken in us this unique experience of depth; he imparted to us his Spirit, his own Spirit, to open our hearts from within to this divine communion and to this Presence....

...The life of prayer and contemplation is simply to realize God's presence in the depth of our being, in the depth of every being, and at the same time beyond all beings, beyond all that is within and all that is without. It is certainly not a way of life that is reserved for those few individuals who are especially called to escape from the world and take refuge in a desert. Contemplation and prayer are the very breath of life, not only for the true disciple of Jesus, but for everyone who has recognized his calling to be human. — *Prayer,* 3–5

# PRAYER — AN ACT OF FAITH

To pray is an act of faith. This does not mean that, in order to pray, we must first confess our faith in more or less abstract terms. No indeed; true prayer is based on the faith, the conviction that God is here, that he is everywhere, that he is in everything, that he is the source from which everything comes and the end (at once immanent and transcendent) to which everything is on the move.

To pray is to take for granted that we live in the mystery of God, that we are immersed in it, and that this mystery envelops us and at the same time extends beyond us on every side. "In him we live and move and have our being" (Acts 17:28). To pray is to realize that the divine mystery in its infinite fullness is at once within us and outside us, that it is totally immanent to our innermost being, and at the same time infinitely transcends it.

But what is meant by this expression, "the mystery of God"? We entirely miss the point if we imagine some high Power or sovereign Personage who sits enthroned far off beyond the sky, governing the universe and the world of mankind at his pleasure — and so one who could be more or less exactly described in terms of a myth or a set of ideas. The mystery of God, as it was revealed to us by Jesus, is the very mystery of the divine life, welling up eternally in the Father, and eternally poured out in the Son and the Spirit, a mystery at once of unity and duality.

The mystery of God is first of all the eternal call of the Father to the Son — the call in which Father and Son essentially *are:* "You are my Son" (Ps. 2:7; see also Mark 1:1–11). It is also the response to this call, the eternal cry of the Son: "Abba, Father!" — the ceaseless prayer of Jesus both on earth and in heaven, a prayer which expresses both the source and the fullness of his love, his sacrifice, and his unending intercession.

The mystery of the divine life is also the universal and all-pervading presence of the Holy Spirit of God. The Holy Spirit is in us, as he is in God, the mystery of unity, of non-duality. He is in us as coming from the Father, as sent to us from the Father, as pouring out in us the eternal love of the Father and the Son. He dwells in us in the innermost recesses of our hearts, "more intimate to us even than we are intimate to ourselves," as Augustine well says. And this presence of the Spirit within the heart of each believer makes them directly present to each other and to every human being — present in their very depths, at the very source of their existence, long before any thought, either loving or divisive, could possibly come into their hearts. In the Spirit each one lives in the very depth of every other person — in the same way as the Father and the Son live from each other and in each other, their "circumincession" in theological language.

— *Prayer,* 12–14

## PRAYER — GOD IS BEYOND FORM

Prayer is to see God, to recognize and adore his presence and his glory in everything — in every being, in every human being, or in any other creature with whom time and the succession of events puts us in contact.

God has no form. He is beyond every form. Precisely for that reason, being free with respect to every form, he can reveal and manifest himself under any form or appearance that he may choose. While no form is capable of signifying him completely, there is no form which he may not adopt in order to reveal himself, and under which he may not at some time ask to be recognized. Those who mock at those divine symbols in the form (for example) of rough stones or of animals which are valued in certain mythologies only show thereby that they themselves are still at the stage of idolatry in their religion, since they link the representation of God to particular forms. *— Prayer,* 27

## GOD IN CREATION

When we raise our eyes to the sky and contemplate the sun and the stars, we are surely praying in truth, if this act is enlivened by faith and enables us to discover the Presence and love of God in them. For it was indeed their slow evolution throughout cosmic ages that prepared the earth to be the cradle of humankind and the place chosen by God for the incarnation of his Son. It is thanks to the light and heat of the sun that life on earth is possible for the children of the heavenly Father, and was possible also for Jesus his First-born, whose divine glance has forever blessed the sun.

To look with eyes of faith at trees and plants, fruit and flowers, birds and animals, all created to assist mankind in their ascent towards God — this also is to contemplate God in the mystery of his manifestation. There is indeed nothing on earth or in the whole universe whose impact on our senses should not blossom into prayer when faith is present. So it was with Jesus; wherever he looked, he contemplated the Father, as he saw everything first of all "in the Father." We might well say also that, through our eyes and all our senses, God himself is contemplating his own creation and rejoicing to find that everything in it is "good...very good" (Gen. 1:10–31).

*— Prayer,* 35–36

## THE PRAYER OF THE NAME

There certainly is no set method or technique, still less any shortcut, whereby we can be brought into the inner sanctuary, to the summit of that "Horeb" which irresistibly draws anyone who has heard the Spirit's call (see 1 Kings 19:8). However, in addition to what has been suggested above, there is one practice whose effectiveness has been recognized for centuries in the spiritual traditions alike of India and of Eastern Christianity.

In India this is called *namajapa,* the prayer of the Name. It consists of the continual repetition of the name of the Lord in one or other of its traditional forms; either the name by itself, for example, "Rama" or "Hari" or "Krishna"; or else an invocation which contains the name, for example, *Om namah Shivaya,* "Glory to Shiva." Some people decide that they will recite a given number of mantras[3] and keep count of them on a kind of rosary containing 108 beads. Others prefer to set apart a fixed time every day when they will repeat the mantra without stopping. Yet others, especially those who have practiced *namajapa* over a long period, do not care either to keep count or to limit the time; they simply go about with the sacred name continually on their lips and in their heart, and sometimes continue to whisper it even during a conversation, interrupting it only when obliged to give an answer. As far as possible, the Name is given by a guru. Sometimes there is one particular name to which the guru initiates any worthy disciple who applies to him — as in the well-known case of Swami Ramdas. Sometimes the guru himself chooses a particular mantra for the disciple, in accordance, at least theoretically, with the aptitude and needs of the one whom he is initiating into the prayer.

Among Christians the nearest equivalent of the Hindu *namajapa* is what is called in the Oriental Christian tradition "the Jesus Prayer." Here too the practice is either a simple repetition of the name of Jesus, or else the use of a longer invocation containing the sacred Name. In these days the most widely used

---

3. *Mantra:* a formula of prayer or invocation. The verses of the Vedas are called mantras. The sense of "mantra" as a magical formula or incantation is secondary.

invocation is: "Lord Jesus, Son of the living God, have mercy on me, a sinner."

In this Christian prayer of the Name we are immediately struck by the stress on our sinful condition and our need for forgiveness. This constant prayer for forgiveness, which is equally characteristic of the whole liturgy of the church, does not however in any way indicate a morbid concern with one's spiritual state, as is sometimes held. Rather it is one way of expressing a deeply personal experience of the love of God and the realization that in forgiving us he reveals most fully his love and almighty power. In the last analysis, to pray for forgiveness unites us with the deepest level of the divine mystery.

Hindu prayer is different. Sometimes, no doubt, the Hindu also prays for forgiveness and for divine help...but most frequently he is content simply to praise and adore: *Om namah Shivaya* (Glory to Shiva), *Om namah Narayanaya* (Glory to the "Son of Man"). Here too it would be improper to find in this almost exclusive stress on adoration the attitude of a proud Pharisee who feels no need to beg for divine forgiveness. At least in those who are truly spiritual, it is rather the sign of total self-forgetfulness and of lack of concern for all that affects them personally — in Christian terms, the complete trust of a child who knows that his father is caring for his needs and whose only personal wish is to continue gazing at him. Indeed, once God has been known in truth, how could anyone in the Presence of Most High give any thought to himself or his own affairs?

The Christian prayer of the Name comes from a very ancient tradition. Its origin can be traced back to the Egyptian monks; St. John Climacus also speaks of it in his *Ladder of Perfection*. Later on, the monks of Mount Athos practiced it diligently. It was the soul of the Hesychast movement; among its best known champions we need only mention Simeon the New Theologian and Gregory Palamas. In recent centuries its influence has spread very widely among Orthodox Christians, especially in Russia.

The form of the prayer has varied widely at different periods, although in our day the invocation most commonly takes the form quoted above. But in whatever form it appears, it is undoubtedly the finest fruit of the ancient practice of brief ejaculatory prayer, which was strongly advocated by the Desert Fathers. Some of them spent their time crying out to God the *Miserere* ("Have mercy on me, O Lord!" Ps. 51:1). Others had a special devotion to the first verse of Psalm 70, which later took its place at the opening of the Divine Office. "Be pleased, O God, to deliver me; make haste, O Lord, to help me!" In the case of others the constant prayer was the *Trisagion* in either of its forms: the "Holy, holy, holy is the Lord!" of Isaiah's vision (6:3), or the "Holy is God! Holy and Almighty! Holy and Immortal!" of the Oriental liturgies. All these prayers have this in common — each is a very brief act of prayer or praise to God, continually repeated and always the same, aimed at fixing the mind on the Lord and making an uninterrupted offering of love and adoration. — *Prayer*, 95–98

## THE PRIMACY OF CONTEMPLATION

The time must come when the Christian, instead of simply keeping step with man's slow advance towards self-realization, will attend to the gentle summons of the Spirit mediated to him by the ancient sages of the East and will allow the Spirit to carry him away within to the abyss of the self. Then God will be able to work on him in those depths of his being which effectively control him, instead of merely at the level of sense and of those other faculties which man, always too grudgingly, makes available to his action. Contemplation will then once more be given its place of primacy in the church, not merely by the religious Orders and by those who are dedicated to the acosmic life, but in the heart of everyone who seeks to make progress in the ways of the Spirit. Whatever harvest the church gathers in the hearts of contemplatives will be available for all its members. Slowly but surely their experience of the depths of the self and of God will be diffused around them, bringing illumination and enrichment. Human society will inevitably be transformed and at last aroused by Christian seers who have that essential fire at their hearts, will become Christian in the full sense of the Gospel. Christian unity, which is so deeply desired and yet remains unattainable so long as men insist on working for it only at the level of intellect, will then come to pass of itself, as Christians will have reached in themselves that place where they are one with God and with their brothers within that very unity which God has in his own Self (John 17:21).

Nothing less than this wonderful foreshadowing of the destiny of the church is contained in the assertion of the transcendent value of *advaita*, and with it of the *sanatana dharma*, with which the Christian is met when he comes into contact with a spiritual Hindu. — *Saccidananda*, 72–73

## ADVAITIC PRAYER

I am supposed to give here some sort of introduction, or initiation, into advaitic or Upanishadic prayer. This is really a challenge, or rather, an impossible task, and this for two fundamental reasons.

First, truly speaking, there is no such thing as advaitic *prayer*. *Advaita* is the central teaching of the Upanishads, and no prayer remains possible for him who has realized the truth of the Upanishads. The equivalent of what is called in monotheistic religions the "experience of God" has here nothing to do with any notion of God whatsoever, for the duality which makes it possible for man to think of himself as standing in front of God has disappeared in the burning encounter with the Real, *sat*.

There is also another reason which makes anyone who is asked to speak on the Upanishads thoroughly uncomfortable. Upanishadic teaching is not a matter of formulations — notions and propositions — which could be transmitted, i.e., taught or received as such. Upanishadic formulations have no other function than to lead to an *experience*. This experience is not prayer, meditation, or contemplation in the commonly accepted sense. It is a kind of consciousness, an awareness to which man finds himself raised beyond the reach of any of his faculties, hearing, seeing, feeling or even thinking:

> There the eye goes not, speech goes not, nor the mind.
> We know not, we understand not how anyone could
>     teach it.
> Other indeed it is than the known and moreover above
>     the unknown.
> Thus we have heard from the ancients who have explained
>     it to us.
> —*Kena Upanishad* 1.3, *Further Shore* 105[4]

## OM

The OM which our *rishis* heard resounding in their
    souls, when they descended to the greatest depths in
    themselves,
deeper than their thoughts and deeper than all their desires,
in the existential solitude of Being.

---

[4]. First published in *Clergy Monthly* (Delhi) 38 (December 1974): 474. Written in English for the Monastic Congress held in Bangalore in 1973.

The OM which sounds in the rustling of leaves shaken by
    the wind,
the OM which howls in the storm
and moans in the gentle breeze,
the OM which roars in the rushing torrent
and the gentle murmur of the river flowing peacefully down
    to the sea,
the OM of the spheres making their way across the sky,
and the OM that throbs at the core of the atom.

That which sings in the song of birds,
that which is heard in the call of beasts in the jungle,
the OM of people laughing and the OM of their sighs.
the OM that vibrates in their thoughts and in all their
    desires,
the OM of their words of warfare, of love, or of trade,
the OM that Time and History utter on their way,
the OM uttered by Space when entering into Time.

This OM suddenly burst out, whole and entire,
in a corner of space and at a point of time,
in its indivisible fullness,
when in Mary's womb was born as Son of man,
the Word, the Son of God.     — *Diary*, 189–90

## THE PRAYER OF SILENCE

Now if something has passed in this long discourse by the way of words, yet beyond words, if you have *heard* in the words of the Upanishads some echo of what the Spirit has certainly whispered in your heart when you sat in contemplation of the mystery of the Father and the Son, then you will discover by yourselves the secret of what is called the advaitic or Upanishadic prayer. It can be summed up in one Hebrew phrase of

Psalm 65, which Jerome translates: *silentium tibi laus.* Silence is praise for you. Silence in prayer, silence in thanksgiving, prayer and adoration, silence in meditation, silence inside and outside as the most essential preparation for this stillness of the soul in which alone the Spirit can work at his pleasure. In the old tradition of Vedic *yajna* [ritual sacrifice] four priests had to sit around the *vedi,* or altar. One of them had the function of performing the rite and meanwhile of repeating the mantras of the Yajurveda. Another was in charge of chanting the hymns of the Silmaveda. The third invoked the devas and recited the *suktas* of the Rigvedi. But the fourth one, the *brahmana* priest par excellence, was to remain silent, whispering as it were without any interruption an almost inarticulate OM. Yet it was that silent OM which was considered as the thread uniting all the different parts of *yajna* and giving to the whole its definitive value.

In the universal canticle which is incessantly ascending towards God from all the quarters of heaven and earth, there is a place, and surely a pre-eminent one, for the praise of the silent OM, and the church cannot afford to be without her silent monks and chiefly hermits, who beyond all rites and all words, whisper in her name and in the name of the whole of mankind and all creation that same silent OM. All petitions are comprised in this silent prayer, for such silence reaches as it were the very origin from which all things proceed from the Father in his eternal Son. All adoration, all thanksgiving, all prayers are comprised as well in this silence, for this silence is one with the silence of the Father from which sounds forth eternally the unique glory which the Son, the Word, is to the Father.

Such silence however is not a self-imposed silence, but a silence, we can say, which is imposed by the Self, the Spirit. One can never forget that the Spirit leads man freely and that no one can ever know or ask the Spirit from whence he comes and where he goes. He can equally make even the *muni* burst eventually into canticles of joy, even dance like David in front of the ark.

Anyhow, the main thrust of spiritual discipline and ascetic life should be to prepare man for the stillness of his faculties where he can be at the full disposal of the Spirit. Such a silence is certainly inconsistent with a life of agitation inward or outward. Yet this stillness is at such a transcendent level in man's spirit that it is not at all incompatible with the normal working of mind and body in the individual and social spheres. To reach such quiet, intensive practice of the meditation of silence is extremely useful for most people. This meditation however has nothing to do with the consideration of diverse aspects of the divine mystery either through imagination or through abstract reflection. It consists in fixing the mind as it were on this point of our awareness, of our self, which is beyond the constant passing of time and succession of surrounding happenings.

The practice of simple yoga is helpful: so is also the use of *namajapa*. Yet all these are only aids — temporary aids. Mantras and *japa* slowly become simplified and even disappear by themselves. OM alone remains, OM *tat sat*, and the OM which is uttered merges finally into the OM which is pure silence.

That is all.

The Christian will say: it is the eternal awakening of the Son to the Father in the *advaita* of the Spirit.

— *Further Shore,* 117–18

# 9

# Awakening

ॐ

*For most of his years in India Abhishiktananda was seeking Enlightenment, satori, or, the word he more often used, Awakening. His final awakening came in the form of a heart attack, but he had been thinking and writing about it for years before that. The fact that this was written some twenty years before he himself attained enlightenment shows how very articulate it is possible to be, even before reaching the full experience.*

## SATORI

One who has attained *satori*, anyone who has been enlightened, continues to see grass as green and the sky as blue, to consider rice as something to eat and cloth as something to wear, and the train as a means of transport. What he is liberated from is the relationship to "himself." Dear ones are no less loved, but there is no longer the least attachment, the least turning back on "himself." God is then known, loved, in himself and no longer in the self of the knower. But this liberation of "himself" and the others and everything else has as its essential, paramount condition the liberation of himself into the Self in itself.... It is only when the *self* sinks into the Self that the world is likewise freed from this self which gives it a cloak as appallingly ugly as the bits of cloth hung on images of Nataraja.

—July 19, 1952, *Diary*, 50

*Awakening is not for the timorous, not for those who want to keep their lives in tidy compartments. It means being open — to loss, to nakedness, to the unexpected, to the formless. It might involve a complete loss of security; it might involve anything at all. It is a dangerous path.*

## DAZZLED

Neither meditation nor concentration. Being there, simply. Sometimes appeals to Christ, to whom I can no longer give any name. Yet I am well aware that he is the most inward mystery, of which the resurrection has caused all forms to explode. He is now the *keshi*, the *Ekarishi*, the amorous Krishna, the dancing Shiva, the Awakened one. All has been taken away — and likewise all that sense of security for the future which has attached to a physical or mental form. That is the real *rupa* (formless.) Not one which is abstracted or imagined, but one into which you are plunged head over heels, completely dazzled.

—MC, October 4, 1971, *Life*, 353

*The following was written shortly before Abhishiktananda died, when he was in a nursing home at Indore under the loving care of Mother Théophane.*

## ONLY FOR THE STRONG

I am tired of Indore, and it needs all Mother Théophane's good humor to prevent me from going under. As she says, I come in the category of "bogged down saints"!...Vedantin experience just as much drains people and is just as dangerous as drugs or psychoanalysis. We usually live on its fringe, like flies which content themselves with the crumbs surrounding the cake. We should only allow very strong people to get involved in it. Yet that is where the only salvation is to be found! So long as we have not accepted the *loss* of all concepts, all myths — of Christ, of the church — nothing can be done! Everything has to spring up anew from the depths, like the Christ who appeared to you the other day at Ranagal in a new Grünewaldine light. It is probably better for most people to pass the *Shakti* by than to be a carrier of it without realizing it. But some are capable of it. It is for them that I should like to have a place beside the Ganges to receive them.   — MC, October 26, 1973, *Life,* 358

## THE PRESENT MOMENT

To refuse the total gift of yourself to others means refusing to be yourself. It is in giving that you become yourself — once more the marvelous myth of the Trinity. But a self-giving that does not alienate the self.

A total depth of exchange in the present moment. The eternity of this exchange lived in the present, without snatching at a future which invariably makes you fall back to the level of pluralism and is a falling away from lived *advaita*....The cosmic *keshi* of the Rig Veda can make his way through the world totally indifferent to everything, looking neither to the right nor to the left; and he can just as well make his way with a smile for all, radiating the life of interchange, as God does when passing through time without leaving his eternity, shedding abroad his love everywhere without leaving his solitude. Ready for everything, and free from all limitation.

— MC, April 5, 1973, *Life,* 327, quoted in SETU, no. 26

## BEYOND ALL SIGNS

...I smile when I see you now so interested in giving a form to the formless. That is just what cults, myths, theologies have done since the beginning.... You need a sign in order to possess your freedom! Oh the infinitely free man who needs a sign that he is beyond all signs!...I am indeed a little to blame for all this. I have talked to you too much and have put ideas into your head — ideas of silence!

...Whoever talks about *jivanmukti* [liberation during one's lifetime], about realization, etc., shows that he has not understood anything at all. Whoever expects an "experience," so that he can say that he is "realized," knows nothing about anything. There is nothing to be renounced, nothing to be released from...Meditation is not a means. For there is no means — neither meditation nor rite nor gnosis nor guru nor scripture.

—MC, April 18 and April 23, 1973,
*Life,* 331–22, quoted in SETU, no. 25

*Abhishiktananda lived for only five months after his heart attack, and for most of the time he was very weak. So his thoughts on what was happening to him are not in books or articles, but in his letters and his* Spiritual Diary. *The following are extracts from letters he wrote to Murray Rogers, who was by then living in Jerusalem and unable to visit him.*

*Abhishiktananda lived and died as a Christian, but he knew that awakening itself took him beyond his religion as normally understood. This made him very concerned as to whether he could any longer speak for the average Christian.*

The more I go the less able I would be to present Christ in a way which could be still *considered* as "Christian." I can start with "Christ" only if my approach is "notional," by ideas. For Christ is first an "idea" which comes to me from outside. Even more after my "beyond life/death experience" of July 14, I can only aim at awakening people to what "they are." Anything about God or the word or any religion which is not based on the deep I-experience is bound to be simply "notion," not existential. From that awakening to self comes the awakening to God — and we discover marvelously that Christ is simply this awakening on a degree of priority rarely if ever reached by man.

Yet I am interested in no *christo-logy* at all. I have so little interest in a Word of God which will awaken man within history.... The "Word of God" comes home to *my* own "present"; it is that very awakening which is my self-awareness. What I discover above all in Christ is his "I AM." I sometimes said jokingly that my next book's cover design would be an "atomic mushroom." There remains only the Ah! of the Kena Upanishad. Christ's experience in the Jordan — Son/Abba — is a wonderful Semitic equivalent of *tat tvam asi/aham Brahma asmi*. Of course I can make use of the Christ experience to lead Christians to an "I AM" experience, yet it is this I AM experience which really matters. Christ is this very mystery "that I AM"; and in this experience and existential knowledge all christo-logy has disintegrated. It is taking to the end the revelation that we are "sons of God."

There is only one Son; each of his manifestations is both *one* and *unique*. So what would be the meaning of a "Christianity-colored" awakening? In the process of awakening all this coloration cannot but disappear (the atomic mushroom). If at all I had to give a message, it would be the message of "Wake up," "arise," "remain aware" of the Katha Upanishad. The coloration might vary according to the audience; but the essential goes beyond. The discovery of Christ's I AM is the ruin of any

Christian theology. For all notions are burned within the fire of experience. Perhaps am I a little too Cartesian, as a good Frenchman. And perhaps others might find a way out of the atomic mushroom. I feel too much, more and more, the blazing fire of this I AM, in which all notions about Christ's personality, ontology, history etc. have disappeared. And I find his real mystery shining in every awakening man, in every mythos.... The only message I could give now is too much burning to be given except with people whom the Spirit might send near me, as he did in the case of Marc. So you realize the dilemma in which I find myself whenever I am asked to speak on Christian interiority and contemplation. — MR, September 2, 1973

... Really a door opened in heaven when I was lying on the pavement. But a heaven which was not the opposite of earth, something which was neither life nor death, but simply "being," "awakening"... beyond all myths and symbols. And finally I believe that coronary attack was only a part, but an essential one, of a whole process of grace. If we meet some time I will tell you the whole wonderful story; till then, *magnificate Dominum mecum*. In the joy of God always.

— MR, September 10, 1973

... Again, if my message could really pass, it would be free from any "notion" except just by the way of "excipient." The Christ I might present will be simply the I AM of my (every) deep heart, who can show himself in the dancing Shiva or the amorous Krishna! And the kingdom is precisely this discovery ... of the "inside" of the Grail!... The awakening is a total explosion. No church will recognize its Christ or itself afterwards. And precisely for that (reason), no one likes the "atomic mushroom." — MR, October 4, 1973

## EXTRACTS FROM ABHISHIKTANANDA'S *SPIRITUAL DIARY*

It is clear from my recollections, from my conversations at the time, from the letters I then wrote, that I lived my heart attack in the first place as a marvelous spiritual adventure.

The center of the intuition that impressed itself on me during those very first days [after July 14] was that the Awakening is independent of any situation whatever, of all the pairs of opposites [*dvandvas*], and first of all of the *dvandva* called life/death.

One awakes everywhere and once for all, and the awakening cannot be confused with what one sees at the moment of the awakening, and therefore with that through which one becomes conscious that one is awake.

The first night was filled with difficult dreams, but not nightmares. I was being led from cave to cave — at different altitudes, 9,000, 11,000, 13,000 feet. The snows of Kashmir were mixed up with the banks of the Ganges. And I was constantly answering: The awakening has nothing to do with "testing oneself" against increasingly difficult life situations. It comes about in any circumstances. At every moment of life, in fact in every circumstance, *I wake up*.

There was also during those nights an acute sense of the smallness of the body, from head to foot. Hard to be convinced that this minimum of matter is enough to support consciousness.

After some days there came to me, as if it were the marvelous solution to an equation: I have found the Grail. And that is what I keep saying and writing to anyone who can grasp the figure of speech. The quest for the Grail is basically nothing else than the quest for the Self. A single quest, that is the meaning of all the myths and symbols. It is yourself that you seeking through everything. And in this quest you run about everywhere, whereas the Grail is here, close at hand; you only have to open your eyes. And that is the finding of the Grail in its ultimate truth, Galahad's direct sight of the inside of the vessel, and no longer just being fed by the Grail which mysteriously passes through the hall, nor even drinking from the Grail....

In those weeks of grace I got the very clear impression that a "new lease" on life had been given me, something beyond the span allotted to me by "life," and that I have no right to misuse it. This grace of awakening — of returning to life — is not for my sake but for others. It was so clear: to announce the discovery of the Grail, to tell people: "Arise, Purusha!" (Katha Upanishad 3, 14), discover the Grail. Look, it is in the depth of yourself, it is the very "I" that you are saying in every moment of conscious life, even in the depth of your consciousness when you dream or sleep. A life from now on that is at the service of this Awakening. How it will be done — about that I have no idea. But it was very clear that for me there has been a fundamental break in my life.

After a few weeks routine naturally took over again, but the insight of those days of grace is always a light that shines within.

This is the culmination of the intuition that struck me in January: "Everything has become clear." There is only the Awakening. All that is "notional" — myths and concepts — is only its expression. There is neither heaven nor earth; there is only Purusha, which I am....

I had such a clear sense of a struggle within me between the angel of death and the angel of life. This "impulse to death" had been pursuing me for a long time. I had often said in recent years that I was living under the sign of Death, but that was quite different from what happened in June–July.

The first day when this showed itself was June 29, that afternoon when Nirmal was singing to Marc and myself the lament "Arunachala Shiva." I could not bear any more. Though I was

*Awakening*

not clearly aware of it, it was like being finally mastered by Arunachala's pillar of fire, a *mythos* in which I lived many of the events of the great week (July 10–18). That funeral chant that accompanied the "passing" of Ramana. The definitive summons of Arunachala. That day in the evening, after the magnificent interview with Chidanandaji — during which once again all three of us endlessly chanted "Arunachala Shiva" — on leaving I was as though seized with giddiness and had to lean on the handrail of the stairs....

...During the day of July 10 I felt very strongly coming to me as it were rites of handing over to M., to free him from his state of discipleship, to make him a "master...." Our farewells on the 14th, which spontaneously took the form of the great departure, *mahaprasthana.*

I felt all the ensuing days as if *Mrityu* [Death] wanted me, was claiming me... and yet, without my feeling it, there was that, the angel of life, the urge to live that was fighting against the death-urge. The circumstances, so manifestly providential, that surrounded my attack. Something within me that was struggling so that I should *survive,* in opposition to that which was struggling within me to carry me off.

I understood the Hindu imagery of the servants of *Yama* [Death] — the story of Savitri[1] — the jaws of Death of the Gita, the jaws of Sheol of the psalms of David.

I lived with intensity the Katha Upanishad, the encounter of Naciketas with Mrityu [Death]. The liberation of the Kumara (son) much less in the first of the boons granted than in the discovery of the third boon. That there is neither life nor death, as I was singing in this verse:

> *na jayate na mriyate kagcit!*
> *na kuta jata na kagcin babhriva...*

---

1. Savitri: a heroine of the *Mahabharata* who rescued her husband, Satyavam, from death as a result of her arguments with Yama, the god of Death.

> No one is either born or dies!
> nor is he born from anywhere, nor
> does he become anyone.
> (Inspired by Katha Upanishad
> 11, 18 and Gita 11, 20)

And all that made me discover myself at a level that went so far beyond all sensations. Seeing myself so weak, so incapable of thought and movement, I became free from my identification with that *myself* which previously used to think and will, used to move about and was anxious about all and sundry. Disconnection. All that consciousness with which I usually moved was no longer mine, and yet I myself still continued to be....

Another intuition, or rather another form of the single intuition, that affected me in those days was: *a-loka*. My freedom, my disconnection from every *loka* — situation, even from the *loka* — situation of life/death. To Be, free from all situations, physical, psychological, spiritual, or religious. Free from every situation — any ascetic setting, any form of asceticism, any form whatever. To find oneself, recover oneself in one's original purity-nakedness.

*September 12*
*The Trinity.* There is within me the source and the non-source, and that is not two. The trinitarian mystery is the revelation of my own depth. Jesus has lived this depth — called divine-human — at an intensely deep level.

Greek speculation made this into abstractions; these abstractions, brought to the concrete level of average intelligence, became modalism or tritheism.

The Trinity can be understood only in the experience of *advaita*. The Trinity is an experience.... It is only discovered in the lucidity of the inner gaze. Jesus has lived this agonizing — and fulfilling — experience of *advaita*. *Advaita*, we call it, in order to try to get beyond the common idea — received from our social environment — of God and oneself, of oneself and others. That is the experience of duality which regards one's skin as the boundary between oneself and other people — and which branches out on the basis of this experience of the "skin." Whereas this experience, though divided into two by the skin — is only one. For the experience of oneself, the foundation of everything and the background, the infrastructure of everything, is only one. Jesus revealed to the human being what he is, what everyone is.

The Trinity is the ultimate mystery of oneself. But in the very depth of this discovery of the Self-Trinity there lies the paradox: in the mystery of the non-source, who still speaks of the Source? It is only at the level of the Source, of the trickle of water springing up, that we speak of what is beyond. In the beyond there is no beyond. It simply is, *etad vai tad!* That, just that!

The Awakening is paradoxically: to awake to what is beyond, and to fall asleep to oneself, to what falls short of it. The Awakening is to enter into a total sleep. But once again, only from this side can we speak of sleep, and equally of Awakening! The Awakening at the level of anyone who has consciousness is precisely to lose oneself, to forget oneself. The Awakening is the shining out of the splendor — in splendor — of the non-awakening of the eternal not-born. The non-awakening, the not-born is manifested by a-what? — a brilliance, a light, a glory that envelops everything, transcends everything, that seizes one and takes one beyond everything. A sense of *"Beyond,"* of the Beyond....

The gift of wisdom, a deep connaturality, an explosion which one who has "felt" cannot evade....     — *Diary,* 385–88

## THE ONLY REAL SELF

The Spirit blows where he wills. He calls from within; he calls from without. May his chosen ones never fail to attend to his

call! In the desert or the jungle, just as much as in the world, the danger is always to fix one's attention upon oneself. For the wise man, who has discovered his true Self, there is no longer either forest or town, clothes or nakedness, doing or not-doing. He has the freedom of the Spirit, and through him the Spirit works as he wills in this world, using equally his silence and his speech, his solitude and his presence in society. Having passed beyond his "own" self, his "own" life, his "own" being and doing, he finds bliss and peace in the Self alone, the only real Self, the *parama-atman*. This is the true ideal of the *sannyasi*.
— *Further Shore*, 16, quoted in SETU, no. 17

## I AM

A person dies of the experience of the infinite (*anata*)
   beyond the beyond —
      Brahman.
Dead, dead, in becoming Brahman, the All,
   Brahman *sarvam*.
Yes that is true,
   being absorbed in this Source!

The Lord has said to me: *Today* I beget you.

O this Purusha of glory [*tejomayah*],
   before the creation of the worlds,
   in their creation
   the golden embryo
      all!
This Purusha in the golden embryo
   who is born unborn [*a-ja*],
   who comes in every birth.
      Oh! But it is myself!

Golden-colored beyond the womb
Oh! When he reveals himself,
when the sun explodes,
the end of the world,
then *I am*.

—May 11, 1972, Diary, 349
quoted in SETU, no. 22

## BEYOND WORDS

The mystery of Christ and of the Father is *beyond words*, more even than that of the *atman*, the *prana*, the Spirit. You can only speak of it in parables, and the meaning of the parable is beyond the words used. —MC, June 3, 1972, Life, 303

One who knows several mental (or religious or spiritual) languages is incapable of absolutizing any formulation whatever — of the gospel, of the Upanishads, of Buddhism, etc. He can only bear witness to an experience — about which he can only stammer....

—April 30, 1973, Diary, 380, quoted in SETU, no. 19

*Also of interest*

## The Cave of the Heart
*The Life of Swami Abhishiktananda*
Shirley du Boulay
Foreword by Raimon Panikkar
ISBN 1-57075-610-4

"Western and Eastern readers alike will be challenged to discover the extraordinary religious experience of a most extraordinary human beings."
–Ursula King

"Immediately becomes the standard treatment of Swami Abhishiktananda and his era."
–Francis X. Clooney, S.J., Harvard Divinity School

## Spirit of Fire
*The Life and Vision of Teilhard de Chardin*
Ursula King
ISBN 1-57075-1773

SMALL PRESS BOOK AWARD WINNER
WITH OVER 100 PHOTOGRAPHS

"This may be the book to hook a new generation on the religious power of Teilhard's vision of divine presence in matter and the evolving universe."
–Elizabeth A. Johnson, CSJ

"From the viewpoint of our present understanding of the universe it could be said that Teilhard is the most significant Christian theologian since Saint Paul."
—Thomas Berry

Please support your local bookstore or call 1-800-258-5838.
For a free catalog, please write us at
Orbis Books, Box 308
Maryknoll, NY 10545-0308
or visit our website at www.orbisbooks.com

Thank you for reading *Swami Abhishiktananda*.
We hope you enjoyed it.

*Also in the Modern Spiritual Masters Series*

## *Bede Griffiths*
*Essential Writings*
Selected by Thomas Matus
ISBN 1-57075-200-1

"This anthology is an excellent introduction to the clarity and passion of his life and teaching and will help many learn from this gentle master of the Christian and universal spiritual traditions."
—Laurence Freeman

## *Sadhu Sundar Singh*
*Essential Writings*
Selected by Charles E. Moore
ISBN 1-57075-592-2

"Sadhu Sundar Singh's dramatic encounter with the living Christ, his refusal to clothe his faith with Western trappings, and his absolute devotion to the way of Jesus make for compelling reading. I highly recommend this book."
—Richard J. Foster

## *Anthony de Mello*
*Writings Selected with an Introduction by*
William Dych, S.J.
ISBN 1-57075-283-4

"De Mello's name conjures up storytelling, irrepressible joy, a relentless search for integrity and a desire to help others plumb the depths of God's experience in their lives."
—Megan McKenna

Please support your local bookstore or call 1-800-258-5838.
For a free catalog, please write us at
Orbis Books, Box 308
Maryknoll, NY 10545-0308
or visit our website at www.orbisbooks.com

Thank you for reading *Swami Abhishiktananda*.
We hope you enjoyed it.